Göttinger Studien zur Entwicklungsökonomik
Göttingen Studies in Development Economics
Herausgegeben von / Edited by Hermann Sautter und/and Stephan Klasen

Bd./Vol. 34

PETER LANG
Frankfurt am Main · Berlin · Bern · Bruxelles · New York · Oxford · Wien

Empirical Analysis of Participation Patterns in Microfinancial Markets

Mirko Bendig

Empirical Analysis of Participation Patterns in Microfinancial Markets

The Cases of Ghana and Sri Lanka

PETER LANG
Internationaler Verlag der Wissenschaften

Bibliographic Information published by the Deutsche Nationalbibliothek
The Deutsche Nationalbibliothek lists this publication in the Deutsche Nationalbibliografie; detailed bibliographic data is available in the internet at http://dnb.d-nb.de.

Zugl.: Göttingen, Univ., Diss., 2011

Cover design:
© Olaf Glöckler, Atelier Platen, Friedberg

Gratefully acknowledging financial support
by FAZIT foundation, Frankfurt/M.,
and Ibero-Amerika-Institut
für Wirtschaftsforschung, Göttingen.

D 7
ISSN 1439-3395
ISBN 978-3-631-63238-3

www.peterlang.de

Editor's Preface

In this volume Mirko Bendig contributes to the empirical literature on households' participation in microfinancial services with applications to various forms of microinsurance schemes in Sri Lanka and Ghana. Microinsurances are seen as options, especially for low-income households in developing countries, to reduce the vulnerability or protect these households from the expenditures associated with potentially catastrophic shocks. Therefore, this analysis of the determinants of households' participation in microinsurance schemes is of particular relevance for development research and policy.

The first two essays are concerned with the interdependencies between participation in different microfinancial services. In the first essay, Bendig argues that a household's decision to take up loans, savings products and insurances are interrelated for various reasons, i.e. whether the participation in microinsurance schemes substitutes each other or is reinforced by the use of other forms of microfinancial services, such as microcredits or microsavings. Therefore, the participation in microinsurance schemes and other financial services are simultaneously estimated using household survey data from Ghana. Hence, the essay addresses the shortcoming in previous academic papers to investigate participation in one type of microfinancial services separately from the use of other services. Furthermore, the essay is the first to estimate the determinants of micro life insurance participation in a sub-Saharan African country, which allows a detailed analysis of the characteristics of the user and non-user of micro life insurance.

The second essay investigates the cumulative participation in microfinancial services using household survey data from Sri Lanka. Here, Bendig assumes that low financial capability leads to a household's limited ability to respond to risk, to its use of a less diversified range of microfinancial services and thus generating a higher level of vulnerability. To demonstrate the cumulation in the use of microfinancial services, the essay estimates the determinants for the three different types of microfinancial services by separate probit models for each financial service on household survey data from Sri Lanka, followed by an ordered probit model to determine the factors affecting a household's decision to participate in no, only one, two or all three different types of microfinancial service. In this way, Bendig finds, in contrast to the Ghanaian case and other academic contributions, that microfinancial service uptake is not seen as an additional risk in Sri Lanka.

In the third essay, Bendig focuses on the question whether micro life insurance participation is also motivated by the desire to leave bequests. Although

Bendig presents, analogous to the first essay for Ghana, the determinants of the participation in micro life insurance, the essay extends the literature in this field significantly by taking explicitly into account whether the bequests are intended or strategic. Interestingly, the essay finds that households' micro life insurance participation correlates with measures of intended bequest motives for protection reasons in Sri Lanka. By doing so, this finding indicates to what extent micro life insurance may contribute to the security of low-income households. This is of particular interest for development research, as the risk of death is – besides health – identified as the most severe hazard in insurance demand research for developing countries.

The fourth essay investigates different sequential steps of the household's microinsurance participation decision and the joint analysis of micro life, health and other forms of microinsurance participation using the same Sri Lankan data set as in the two previous essays. Bendig argues that members of an MFI have better access to and are more likely to participate in microinsurance schemes due to unobservable characteristics of their MFI membership. Furthermore, the essay argues that the participation in one microinsurance type is reinforced by the availability of other types of insurance by estimating the determinants of a household's decision to participate in different types of microinsurance using multivariate probit models. By doing so, Bendig shows that the decision to buy health and life insurance are positively correlated with each other.

These essays all make important contributions to the empirical literature on households' participation in microfinancial services and especially various forms of microinsurance schemes in developing countries, so that I am pleased that this book has been included in our series of studies on economic development.

Author's Preface

First of all, I would like to thank my supervisor Prof. Stephan Klasen for accepting me as a doctoral student, giving me the chance to write my thesis and especially for his patience and academic support. I am also very grateful to Jun.-Prof. Dr. Jann Lay for his helpful comments to my research.

Next, I wish to thank Thankom Arun, who co-authored the chapters on Sri Lanka, for his support and productive discussions which were of really unpayable value to finish this thesis. I would like to express my sincere thanks to my co-authors Susan Steiner and Lena Giesbert, who co-authored the chapter on Ghana, for their help and the unique experience of conducting the field survey in Ghana. Furthermore, I am also very thankful to many of my colleagues from evers & jung.

My special thank goes to Johanna for taking care of me and all the special moments in the last three years and in particular for believing in me and whatever I am doing. Furthermore, I would like to express a very big thank to my family, especially to my parents, and Nadine and Karsten, for their persistent support and great care.

I am also very grateful to Moritz (for "supervising" my private life), Sascha, Dennis, Andreas, Thomas F., Kai, Susi and Stefan, who supported me in many ways and especially above all in non-ecomomic things. Last, I would like to express a very big thank to all other people who helped me directly and indirectly with my thesis and who I forgot to explicitly mention here.

Author's Preface

Contents

List of Tables

List of Abbreviations

ADB	Asian Development Bank
ALMAO	All Lanka Mutual Assurance Organization
APEs	Average Partial Effects
CBO	Community Based Organization
CGAP	Consultative Group to Assist the Poor
FASs	Funeral Aid Societies
GDP	Gross Domestic Product
GHK	Geweke-Hajivassiliou-Keweke
GLICO	Gemini Life Insurance Company
GTZ	Deutsche Gesellschaft für Technische Zusammenarbeit
IBSL	Insurance Board of Sri Lanka
ILO	International Labour Organisation
IMF	International Monetary Fund
LDC	Least Developed Country
MEs	Marginal Effects
MFI(s)	Microfinance Institution(s)
MIX	Microfinance Information Exchange
NGO	Non-Governmental Organization
NHIS	National Health Insurance Scheme
OLS	Ordinary Least Squares
PIA	Personal Insurance Adviser
PRFC	Private Finance Research Centre, University of Bristol
RCB(s)	Rural and Community Bank(s)
SANASA	Sanasa Insurance Company
SEEDS	Sarvodaya Economic Enterprises Development Services Ltd.
SML	Simulated Maximum Likelihood
UNDP	United Nations Development Programme
VIFs	Variance Inflation Factors
WDBF	Women's Development Banking Federation
WDF	Women's Development Federation
YASIRU	Yasiru Mutual Fund

Introduction and Overview

> "The accepted human rights are food, shelter, health and education, and the basic responsibility of a society is to make sure that an environment exists so that people can have these things. Employment is also a right, but society can't assure wage-based work for everybody, so the alternative is self-employment. The big financial institutions currently ignore almost two-thirds of the world's population. So I say the right to credit should have the topmost priority on the list of human rights."
>
> (Muhammad Yunus)

This somewhat over-subtle statement of Yunus shows his vision of broadening access to financial services to everybody in the world (Yunus 2003). Due to the fact that only half of the population in many developing countries hold an account with a financial institution, development theorists also see the lack of access to financial markets as critical for generating income and wealth inequality (World Bank 2008). Several reasons for these limited financial markets, i.e. credit, savings and insurance markets, are identified by academics in many developing countries. The first reason why banks are inactive in the field of poor customers is the prevalence of a high number of very small transactions, which leads to far more expensive transaction costs compared to rich customers with significantly larger and fewer transactions, so that these possible target groups are unattractive for normal banks (Armendáriz and Morduch 2010).

Secondly, information asymmetries between financial service providers and possible clients, i.e. moral hazard and adverse selection (Akerlof 1970, Rothschild and Stiglitz 1976, Browne and Doerpinghaus 1993, Cawley and Phillipson 1999, Winter 2000, Abbring et al. 2003), are reasons for the fact that formal-sector financial institutions have such a low profile in low-income communities. In the case of lending, moral hazard arises when the bank cannot observe whether the customers are making the full effort for a successful investment of the loan amount in a project or whether they are engaging in risky behaviour which raises the risk of default (Rothschild and Stiglitz 1976, Cawley and Phillipson 1999, Armendáriz and Morduch 2010, Winter 2000). Therefore, traditional banks require collateral as security for the loan, which the poor typically lack; thus, they are excluded from credit access by their limited liability (Armendáriz and Morduch 2010). Adverse selection arises when banks cannot determine whether the borrower's project is low or high risk or whether one project or borrower is riskier than others (Akerlof 1970, Rothschild and Stiglitz 1976, Browne and Doerpinghaus 1993, Cawley and Phillipson 1999, Armendáriz and Morduch 2010). All borrowers are then charged the same interest rates, so that low-risk borrowers might pay more or refuse to borrow and the banks remain with a loan portfolio of riskier borrowers than average. Due to these inadequate financial markets, "the promise is that microfinance can indeed do better than what exists" (Armendáriz and Morduch 2005: 34); that is, it can reduce transaction costs, avoid information problems through a close relationship with clients and by hiring loan officers out of the related communities, provide incentives or mechanisms such as group loans to compensate for the limited liability, and so ultimately broaden the access to financial services for the poor.

The microfinance movement has its roots in several ideas regarding the provision of banking services to everyone. As an example from developed countries, for instance, the outgrowth of the cooperative banking movement started in the 19th century in Germany, which has since largely targeted banking for everyone, including the provision of access to financial services, in particular credit, to low-income groups for over a century. Nevertheless, the most famous instance and at the same time the impetus for the emergence of microfinance arose in 1976, when Muhammad Yunus, an economist teaching at Chittagong University in the southeast of Bangladesh, started experiments by lending small amounts of money to poor households. These households were located in the village of Jobra close to the University, and Yunus lent them money to run simple business activities. Out of these experiments, he built the Grameen Bank in Bangladesh, and by June 2008, the bank had 7.5 million clients all over Bangladesh (Armendáriz and Morduch 2010). Following the model of the Grameen Bank, microfinance institutions (MFIs) have been built all over the world in the past three decades, based on Yunus' experiments rather than on earlier experiences or standard banking models in developed countries (Armendáriz and Morduch 2010). For this successful innovation, Muhammad Yunus and the Grameen Bank of Bangladesh received the Nobel Peace Prize in 2006, following the International Year of Microcredit celebrated in 2005 by the UN, both of which have significantly raised the public awareness of microfinance.

In developing countries, households and individuals are faced by risky events that threaten their lives, health and property, events such as death, illness, injury and accident (Holzmann and Joergensen 2000, Siegel et al. 2001). Sources of vulnerability include the high correlation of poverty and ill health, the riskiness of agricultural occupations, employment instability within the informal sector, and the general insecurity that arises from weak legal protections (Siegel et al. 2001, Karlan and Morduch 2009). In most of the developing world low-income households are disproportionately vulnerable to risk, as they lack the adequate means to manage or minimise their exposure to risk (Holzmann and Joergensen 2000, Siegel et al. 2001). Similar to any other financial market, such as the credit market, the access to and the provision of insurance is still limited in many developing countries (Roth et al. 2007, World Bank 2008). Hence, the poor depend highly on very costly and mostly insufficient traditional informal coping mechanisms, which are not adequate for smooth consumption (Morduch 1994, Townsend 1995, Dercon 2004). The same is true for the only infrequently provided social security measures in many developing countries (Siegel et al. 2001). Therefore, low-income households are mostly only partially insured against income shocks in developing countries (Morduch 1995, Townsend 1995, Lim and Townsend 1998), so that in the case of shocks to a household's income such as the death of a household member, the poor remain unable to insure against the consumption downturns of such risky events, which in the long run might induce famine or death. In such a case, microfinance promises to provide means which offer consumption smoothing to prevent losses resulting from future hazards, to cope with the present consequences of experienced shocks or to provide help over periods of cyclical downturns.

Initially limited to microcredit, microfinance has become more and more demand-oriented and diversified, as "low-income households can profit through access to a broader set of financial services than just credit" (Armendáriz and Morduch 2005: 147, Zeller and Sharma 2002). Although the idea of microinsurance emerged in the 1990s, the field of microinsurance[1] is still young, but holds the promise of reducing the vulnerability of low-income households to negative shocks and the consequences of these on income and consumption. The concept of insurance is not completely new for low-income households in developing countries, as, due to the low coverage of public social security systems, low-income people traditionally rely on informal risk management and self-insurance strategies in order to protect against the occurrence of risky events (Townsend 1995, Siegel et al. 2001). If the shocks are idiosyncratic and characterized of low frequency, such as the death of a household member, the risk may be insurable, but if the negative shocks are covariate, as in the case of a drought or a flood, the risk is harder to insure or insurance may be limited (Morduch 1995, Townsend 1995, Dercon 2002). Furthermore, the poor use a wide variety of risk coping mechanisms from both informal, such as the exchange of loans between members of an extended family or a community in emergency cases, and formal sources, and base their choice of risk coping behaviour and their participation in any financial service schemes on the information and advice

1 The most common definition of microinsurance is the "protection of low-income people against specific perils in exchange for regular premium payments proportionate to the likelihood and cost of the risk involved" (Churchill 2006: 12)

they get from close-knit networks of households (Townsend 1995, Cole et al. 2009, Armendáriz and Morduch 2010).

The understanding that the poor cannot afford insurance premiums as well as being uninsurable against the wide variety of risks they face, dramatically changed after the emergence of microinsurance, so that microinsurance has the potential to be an important instrument to any poverty reduction strategy (Siegel et al. 2001, Churchill 2006). A high demand for microinsurance, especially for health and life insurance products, is actively promoted because of a lack of efficient risk coping mechanisms in developing countries, but the uptake of microinsurance is still low (Cohen et al. 2005, McCord et al. 2006, Roth et al. 2007). One reason for the limited provision of microinsurance is from the supply-side perspective, namely that providing microinsurance has all the incentive and information problems of providing insurance or credit, i.e. moral hazard and adverse selection (Cawley and Phillipson 1999, Winter 2000, Abbring et al. 2003), high transaction costs and difficult contract enforcement (Armendáriz and Morduch 2010). Furthermore, due to the limited size of the resource pool of vulnerable households, existing microinsurance programmes can cover only a limited range of risks (Siegel et al. 2001). In addition, there is so far no approach in the microinsurance industry that offers a breakthrough comparable to that which group-lending innovation has been for the compensation of the limited liability of the poor in the microcredit provision (Morduch 2006).

On the demand side, in academic and policy makers' circles, the lack of information and understanding of insurance concepts and all their terms and conditions, combined with mistrust in the providing institutions, are generally viewed as significant barriers to higher microinsurance uptake among low-income households in developing countries (Schneider 2005, Chankova et al. 2008, Ginè et al. 2008, Cole et al. 2009). Hence, low-income households still cover the costs of shocks with a wide range of risk management strategies, including financial services from different sources, be these formal, informal or self-insurance. However, microinsurance is a promising approach for social protection and the reduction of the vulnerability of the poor to the consequences of negative shocks, and can thus play a key role as a possible component of an integrated social risk management strategy for the developing world (Siegel et al. 2001).

The contributions in the literature on the determinants of a household's use of financial services in developing countries have long been dominated by the issue of participation in credit schemes (Atieno 1997, Kochar 1997, Jabbar et al. 2002, Nguyen et al. 2002, Pal 2002, Pitt and Khandker 2002, Swain 2002, Zeller and Sharma 2002, Barslund and Tarp 2008), followed, to a lower extent, by that of savings (Gupta 1970, Deaton 1992, Gurgand et al. 1994, Muradoglu and Taskin 1996, Spio and Groenewald 1996, Fafchamps et al. 1998, Kimuyu 1999, Aryeteey and Udry 2000, Kiiza and Pederson 2002, Hoogeven 2003). The attention focus on insurance is still more limited, with several contributions on the demand for informal insurance and risk sharing arrangements (Alderman and Paxson 1994, Morduch 1995, Townsend 1995, Platteau 1997, Dercon 2002, Kurosaki and Fafchamps 2002, Fafchamps and Lund 2003), but only a few studies, using quantitative household survey data, on formal insurance. Among these, there are quantitative studies on micro health (e.g. Asfaw 2003, Jütting 2003, Bhat and Jain 2006, Hamid et al. 2010, Ito and Kono 2010) and on weather or agriculture related microinsurance (e.g. Giné et al. 2008, Cole et al. 2009, Giné and Yang 2009), emphasizing the basis risk, household wealth, credit constraints, risk aversion, trust, endorsement of social networks, hyperbolic preferences, and particular marketing methods as determinants of a household's microinsurance participation in developing countries (Wang and Rosenman 2007, Giné et al. 2008, Cai et al. 2009, Giné and Yang 2009, Cole et al. 2009, Thornton et al. 2009, Ito and Kono 2010). The simple neoclasscial model of participation in rainfall insurance developed by Giné, Townsend and Vickery (2008) is hereby seen as a benchmark model (Cole et al. 2009, Ito and Kono 2010).

In the academic debate on the use of microfinancial services, there is still an urgent need for more empirical analysis of the determinants of the participation in formal microinsurance schemes, which is the underlying motivation of this work. The main objective is to provide new insights into the analysis of a household's microfinancial service participation patterns that might contribute to a better understanding of whether microfinancial services function as efficient risk management strategies for low-income households in developing countries. Consequently, the thesis investigates the nature of the idiosyncratic or covariate shocks low-income households are faced by, which informal and formal risk management strategies are used to cover the consequences of such risky events, what role microinsurance can play as a risk coping mechanism, whether a substantial contribution to poverty reduction can be expected from it, and, finally, why several low-income households contract microinsurance, but others not, and why not. By doing so, the research allows us to examine whether the participation in microinsurance schemes is determined by supply or demand side factors.

On the demand side, a special emphasis will be put on the analysis of the demographic and socioeconomic determinants of the households participating in microinsurance schemes, thus indicating what kind of households participate in such schemes. At the same time, the thesis aims to identify supply-side factors influencing microinsurance provision and in particular why the uptake of microinsurance is still low; for instance, information asymmetries are widely seen as potential explanations for barriers to insurance participation in the literature (Akerlof 1970, Rothschild and Stiglitz 1976, Browne and Doerpinghaus 1993, Cawley and Phillipson 1999, Winter 2000, Abbring et al. 2003). In this way, the work also sheds more light on the underlying open issues and questions in the empirical analysis of microfinancial services on the interdependencies between the participation in different microfinancial service schemes, a household's financial capability level, and its vulnerability (Siegel et al. 2001, Matul 2009).

The four essays which comprise the thesis, and which will be introduced below in more detail, are concerned with the empirical analysis of households' participation in microfinancial services, different types of microinsurance, namely micro life and health insurance, and on the sequential steps of a household's participation decision. Surprisingly, so far no major research has been carried out using household survey data on the participation in micro life insurance in developing countries, although micro life insurance is the most widely provided microinsurance in the world (Roth et al. 2007). While there are some studies, using individual household data for both developed and developing countries, on the participation in formal life insurance (Lewis 1989, Truett and Truett 1990, Browne and Kim 1993, Outreville 1996), all of these use earlier theoretical work on the demand for life insurance as a benchmark (Yaari 1965, Hakansson 1969, Fischer 1973, Lewis 1989). While Lewis (1989) was the first to extend the previous theoretical work including the preferences of the dependents and beneficiaries, i.e. bequest motives, this thesis is the first to use this model to concentrate on underlying motivations of the micro life insurance participation based on intra-household allocation decisions, such as bequest motives, in developing countries.

The thesis considers different countries in different developing regions, these being Ghana from sub-Saharan Africa and Sri Lanka from South Asia. A generalization of the results and the replicability for microinsurance participation patterns in other countries might also be given, as the countries differ in historical, cultural and political background, including in terms of social security systems. In addition, the microfinance sectors and especially the provision of microinsurance differ extensively between these countries. Due to the fact that the microinsurance sector in Sri Lanka is more diversified and developed in terms of availability, coverage and engagement in the market than in Ghana, it might be possible to derive replicable implications and determinants of participation for the better provision of microinsurance for microfinance sectors at different stages of development.

Furthermore, this thesis helps to contribute to the discussion on the influence of microfinance and in particular of microinsurance on poverty reduction and its implications for political promotion, including economic development policy and social protection. From the supply-side perspective, recommendations can be given for the better distribution and marketing of microfinancial services in order to understand whom to provide with these services and how to achieve a higher level of outreach of microfinance, including microinsurance. The thesis can provide new insights into a better understanding of the demand-driven determinants of the poor's participation in microfinancial schemes, and thus give recommendations for how to make the poor more financially capable, such as the promotion of financial and/or insurance education, simple and easily understandable services, trustworthy marketing and distribution measures.

In this thesis both **Essay 1**, based on joint work with Lena Giesbert and Susan Steiner, and **Essay 2**, based on joint work with Thankom Arun, discuss the interpendencies between participation in different microfinancial services, as one major limitation of the previous academic papers is that they investigate participation in one type of microfinancial service, for instance microcredit, separately from the use of microsavings or microinsurance. In contrast to these earlier contributions, **Essay 1** argues that a household's decision to take up loans, savings products and insurance, offered informally or formally, are interrelated for various reasons, e.g. informational advantages or higher financial capability of users over non-users. Therefore, the forms of participation in microinsurance and other financial services are simultaneously estimated in a reduced-form multivariate probit model on household survey data from Ghana. Furthermore, **Essay 1** is the first study estimating the determinants of the uptake of micro life insurance in a sub-Saharan African country to allow a detailed analysis of which households use micro life insurance and which not, and helps to explain why micro life insurance uptake is still low.

The results of **Essay 1** present evidence that there is a mutually reinforcing relationship between the use of micro life insurance and the use of other formal financial services in Ghana. Furthermore, **Essay 1** finds no evidence for a substitution or crowding out effect between the use of informal financial services and the uptake of micro life insurance. **Essay 1** finds that risk averse households as well as households which consider themselves more exposed to risk are less likely to participate in a micro life insurance scheme, so that it is argued that households seem to consider the micro life insurance scheme under study to be risky in itself and not as a risk mitigation measure. There is also an indication of adverse selection and a life cycle effect for microinsurance participation in Ghana.

The **second essay** stresses that the microfinancial service participation of low-income households, i.e. the respective usage of no, one, two or all different types of microfinancial services, gives an indication of the diversification of a household's financial behaviour, in terms of the importance of the risk management strategies in use. Therefore, **Essay 2** assumes that low financial capability leads to a household's limited ability to respond to risk, to its use of a less diversified range of microfinancial services and thus indicates the higher level of vulnerability of the household. To demonstrate this, the determinants for the three different types of microfinancial services are estimated by separate probit models for each financial service on household survey data from Sri Lanka, followed by an ordered probit model to determine the factors affecting a household's decision to participate in no, only one, two or all three different types of microfinancial services. In this way, **Essay 2** aims to derive insights as to whether a higher risk exposure in the past influences a household's decision to diversify its microfinancial service participation. In contrast to earlier contributions in the literature (e.g. Giné et al. 2008) and **Essay 1**, **Essay 2** finds that financial service uptake is not seen as an additional risk in Sri Lanka. Whether a household is more or less likely to use microfinancial services depends highly on the type of shock experienced, whereas the accessibility to one, two or three microfinancial services is determined by the experience of specific hazards, such as the death of a household member in the past. Better off households are still more likely to use microfinancial services than their poorer counterparts in Sri Lanka. In addition, there is evidence for a negative relationship between microfinancial service participation and the lack of a basic level of financial capability, as household heads with no or low educational attendance are negatively associated with a diversified participation in microfinancial services in Sri Lanka.

The **third essay** presents evidence, analogous to **Essay 1** for Ghana, on the determinants of the participation in micro life insurance using probit and tobit models on household survey data from Sri Lanka, so that **Essay 3** is the first study on micro life insurance participation in a South-Asian country. **Essay 3** argues that micro life insurance participation is motivated – besides other socio-demographic and supply-driven determinants – by the policy holder's desire to leave bequests. Therefore, **Essay 3** is the first to evaluate the determinants of micro life insurance participation against the benchmark model of life insurance demand developed by Lewis (1989) and also takes into account whether the bequests are intended or strategic (Tomes 1982, Bernheim et al. 1985, Hurd 1987), which has so far only been analysed in a developed country context. This is of particular interest for the question as to whether and to what extent micro life insurance may contribute to the security of low-income households in the case of the breadwinner's death. By doing so, the work goes beyond the issue of micro life insurance ownership, by using additionally as a dependent variable the premium expenditures indicating the actual amount of insurance coverage purchased. There is evidence that micro life insurance participation correlates with measures of intended bequest motives for protection reasons in Sri Lanka. Furthermore, the estimations of determining factors of micro life insurance participation show both confirmation of and deviation from the Lewis' model predictions in **Essay 3**, as the results indicate, for instance, that the religious inclination of the underlying sample is associated with participation in micro life insurance schemes.

None of the existing contributions in the literature, as the **last paper** of this dissertation, based on work with Thankom Arun, does, emphasize different sequential steps of the household's microinsurance participation decision and the joint analysis of micro life, health and other forms of microinsurance participation using household survey data from Sri Lanka. **Essay 4** argues that members of an MFI have better access to and are more likely to participate in microinsurance schemes due to unobservable characteristics of their MFI membership. Furthermore, we assume that the participation in one microinsurance type is reinforced by the availability of other types of insurance. Therefore, **Essay 4** estimates what determines a household's enrolment in an MFI, and to what extent is a household's microinsurance participation conditional on its MFI enrolment, before finally employing multivariate probit models to estimate the determinants of a household's decision to participate in different types of microinsurance, i.e. life, health, and any other type of insurance. The results of **Essay 4** presents evidence that the participation in life and any other insurance or health and any other insurance are conflicting alternatives. A household's experience of a family related shock is positively associated with participation in micro health insurance schemes. However, microinsurance has not yet succeeded in proportionately reaching the most vulnerable households in Sri Lanka. Furthermore, education and household size are strong determinants of a household's MFI enrolment and microinsurance participation in Sri Lanka.

The Appendices following **Essay 4** contain additional country specific information on the data sets and results of the respective empirical analyses. The Bibliography for all parts is also located at the end of the thesis.

Essay 1

1. Participation in Micro Life Insurance and the Use of other Financial Services

Abstract:

This paper investigates households' decisions to take up micro life insurance and to use other financial services in Ghana. It estimates a multivariate probit model based on household survey data. The results provide evidence for a mutually reinforcing relationship between the use of micro life insurance and the use of other formal financial services. Risk averse households and households who consider themselves more exposed to risk than others are found to be less likely to participate in insurance. This suggests that insurance is considered to be risky. There is also indicative evidence for adverse selection and a life cycle effect in the uptake of micro life insurance.

1.1 Introduction

In recent years, there has been a profound transition in the understanding of microfinance. Academics as well as practitioners have come to realize that "low-income households can profit through access to a broader set of financial services than just credit" (Armendáriz and Morduch 2005: 147). Microcredit long dominated the microfinance market, but many financial institutions have now established deposit accounts – to the extent that the number of deposit accounts is more than double the number of outstanding loans in sub-Saharan Africa today (Lafourcade et al. 2005) – and microinsurance has entered the market in many developing countries. However, since it is a relatively young phenomenon, the spread of microinsurance is still limited. A recent study shows that only about 2.6 percent of the African population living under US$2 per day are currently covered (Matul et al. 2010). Nevertheless, microinsurance is generally seen and promoted as an important financial service for low-income people in developing countries, offering (at least partial) protection in the event of serious shocks, such as death, illness, or natural catastrophes, given the absence of accessible and functioning conventional insurance markets and public social security systems.[2]

---

2 See, for instance, the detailed contributions in Churchill (2006) on the challenges and potentials of microinsurance.

While microcredit and, to a lesser extent, microsavings, have been studied quite extensively, microinsurance has so far received only limited attention in the academic literature. In particular, not much is known about why uptake of microinsurance is still low, even though this is one of the most crucial questions to answer if greater coverage is to be achieved. A number of recent studies have focused on the determinants of housholds' participation in the microinsurance market pointing to the importance of basis risk, household wealth, credit constraints, risk aversion, trust, endorsement from social networks, hyperbolic preferences, and particular marketing methods (Wang and Rosenman 2007, Giné et al. 2008, Cai et al. 2009, Cole et al. 2009, Giné and Yang 2009, Thornton et al. 2009, Ito and Kono 2010).

We argue that households' participation in microinsurance may additionally be related to the use of other financial services, i.e. loans and savings products, and that this may also help to explain low insurance uptake. In fact, we can think of different ways in which insurance, loans and savings may be interrelated. On one hand, it could be that the three services are substitutes for each other. Microinsurance does not enter a vacuum but joins a range of alternative mechanisms, including financial services, which households use in order to share risks and to deal with shocks. To the extent that these mechanisms are, or at least appear to be, efficient strategies, households may tend to continue applying them, which may in turn explain low uptake of microinsurance.

As the literature has shown, household savings often serve an insurance purpose. Such a precautionary motive for savings is in contrast to an accumulation motive, and it is higher when income is uncertain and credit constraints are taken into account (Skinner 1988, Deaton 1989, Eswaran and Kotwal 1989, Zeldes 1989, Besley 1995, Browning and Lusardi 1996, Giles and Yoo 2007, Lee and Sawada 2007, 2010). Credit also often takes on insurance functions if it is used for consumption instead of investment (Eswaran and Kotwal 1989, Zeller 2001). There is a vast literature on risk sharing, including the exchange of loans between members of an extended family or a community in emergency cases, which many authors refer to as informal insurance (Alderman and Paxson 1994, Morduch 1995, 1999, Townsend 1995, Platteau 1997, Dercon 2002). However, credit as insurance is not a feature of the informal financial market alone; it is well applicable to loans on the formal financial market. It is plausible that savings and loans are particularly strongly used as substitutes for insurance when no insurance market exists, as in many developing countries, but we believe there is no reason to expect the motivation for precautionary savings and emergency loans to vanish with the expansion of formal insurance[3].

On the other hand, it could be that the uses of insurance, loans and savings reinforce each other, at least if we think of insurance as being distributed via financial institutions that also provide the respective other services. There are no good theoretically reasons why different financial services should reinforce each other, but in practice this might happen. First, users of one service may simply have an informational advantage over non-users in the sense that they either learn about additional services "by accident" when visiting their respective financial institutions or are deliberately approached and informed by bank staff. Second, users may have a higher level of financial literacy than non-users, that is, a better understanding of how financial services function, and may therefore better recognize the advantages of using another service as well. Third, savings as well as insurance may serve as a kind of collateral for loans, especially among poorer households for which other (asset-based) forms of collateral are unavailable[4]. Fourth, life insurance might be mandatory for getting credit from any of the credit providers, if so, the interrelation between the financial services is by product design, for instance by credit life insurances[5]. Fifth, life insurance only covers the occurrence of death in the household, while savings and credit covers more adverse circumstances beyond it, so that households might use more than one financial service to cover the consequences of all possible future hazards. In all cases, households using at least one service can be assumed to be more likely to start using an additional service than households using no service at all. The fact that a non-negligible share of households in developing countries does not have access to the formal financial market may in fact explain low uptake of microinsurance.

It is the objective of this paper to contribute to the discussion on the demand-side determinants of households' participation in microinsurance. Our approach differs from previous studies in three ways. First, we explicitly take into account that households tend to use more than one financial service and that there may be interconnections between these. It is not a trivial task to consider the uptake of microinsurance and the use of other financial services in an empirical estimation. There is vast scope for endogeneity, as unobserved het-

3 For example, Lee and Sawada (2007) show that US households, which can be assumed to have access to insurance markets in principle, save for precautionary motives to a non-negligible extent.

4 Compulsory savings programmes, so-called "forced savings" is a well-known phenomenon in microfinance markets worldwide (Armendáriz and Morduch 2005).

5 So-called credit life insurances and all other compulsory insurance products are dropped from the analysis, so that we emphasize voluntary insurance uptake.

erogeneity may actually influence households' decisions of uptake of all of the services. Additionally, there may be problems of reverse causality as households without insurance may tend to save more, or take up more loans, in order to deal with future, or past, shocks. Therefore, and in order to capture potential joint underlying decision-making processes, we address the choices of microinsurance, formal savings, informal savings, formal loans, and informal loans simultaneously in a reduced-form multivariate probit model. Such a framework takes into account that the relative probability of uptake of a financial service is influenced by the existence of other alternatives. Another difference to previous studies is that we investigate the uptake of life insurance, whereas earlier studies have concentrated on agriculture, weather index, or health insurance. And third, we present evidence on the uptake of microinsurance in a sub-Saharan African country, which, to our knowledge, is the first study of this kind.

The empirical analysis in this paper is based on cross-sectional data from a survey of 350 Ghanaian households, some of which have purchased a micro life insurance (packaged with a hospitalization benefit, accident coverage and an optional savings scheme). The survey was conducted by the authors in two neighboring small towns (Brakwa and Benin) in the Asikuma/Odoben/Brakwa district of the Ghanaian Central Region in February 2008 in the context of a research project on the uptake of insurance in sub-Saharan Africa.

We find some evidence that there is a mutually reinforcing relationship between the use of micro life insurance and the use of other formal financial services, but no evidence for a substitution or crowding out effect between the use of informal financial services and micro life insurance in Ghana. There is empirical evidence that the use of microinsurance depends not only on the socioeconomic status of households, but also on various other factors, such as households' risk assessment, past exposure to shocks and adverse selection.

The paper is structured as follows. Following this introduction, Section 1.2 presents the particular microinsurance relevant to this paper. Section 1.3 provides a theoretical framework for households' decisions to take up microinsurance. Section 1.4 describes the source of data, including sample selection and external validity. Section 1.5 introduces the outcome and explanatory variables. The estimation strategy is presented in Section 1.6, and the estimation results are shown and interpreted in Section 1.7. Section 0 serves as a conclusion.

1.2 Design and Distribution of the Anidaso Microinsurance Policy

The microinsurance under study here is called Anidaso policy ("anidaso" meaning "hope" in Twi) and is provided by the commercial Gemini Life Insurance Company (GLICO). The Anidaso policy was developed with initial support of CARE International, but GLICO does not receive subsidies of any kind for this insurance today. The policy offers term life insurance up to age 60, accident benefits, and hospitalization benefits (calculated per day spent in hospital) for the policy holder, the spouse, and up to four children. Contributions towards a so-called investment plan, which serves as a savings scheme and pays the accumulated amount at the maturity of the term, can be added on a voluntary basis. We found during our research that most policy holders are actually unaware of the accident and hospitalization benefits and consider Anidaso to be a pure life insurance or, to a lesser extent, a savings device (for retirement)[6]. The policy is specifically targeted at low-income people in both urban and rural areas.

For the sale and distribution of the policy, GLICO started to cooperate in early 2004 with six rural and community banks (RCBs)[7]. It currently collaborates with 20 RCBs, five MFIs and one savings and loan company in six regions of southern Ghana. The number of Anidaso policy holders per financial institution ranges from around 200 to over 1,000, and the total number of policy holders had reached 15,000 by December 2008. In each of the partnering financial institutions, GLICO assigns one Personal Insurance Advisor (PIA), who is in charge of marketing the Anidaso policy and mediating all running operations between the bank and the insurance company. In addition, there is usually a team of a minimum of two sales agents that joins forces with the PIA in the marketing process. The PIA and the sales agents are typically recruited locally, but they are trained at GLICO's headquarters.

GLICO's marketing strategy includes approaching group and opinion leaders in the communities, who are then mobilized to spread the word about the product and to help organize marketing meetings. Furthermore, PIAs and sales

---

6 The fact that GLICO has hitherto only received claims upon death of policy holders but no claims in relation with any of the additional policy components underlines our impression that policy holders consider the Anidaso policy to be a pure life insurance.

7 In general, RCBs are unit banks owned by members of the community. While they do not exclusively target low-income people, their business is by and large microfinance orientated because the majority of the population in their service areas can be classified as low-income (Basu et al. 2004, Steel and Andah 2008).

agents attend group meetings of microfinance groups or other (financial) self-help groups, accompany rural banks' mobile bankers[8], make individual door-to-door marketing rounds and approach visitors at the bank. Less frequently, GLICO holds large and widely announced product launches at community centers and bank offices. Interested individuals can usually apply on the spot.

There are no clearly defined eligibility criteria for policy holders except that they have to be adults below the age of 55 and that they have, or are willing to open up, an account with the local financial institution. This latter condition is necessary because the insurance premiums are directly deducted from policy holders' accounts; or from group accounts (if policy holders are organized in groups)[9]. No detailed health check or information on the health condition of applicants or other household members is required[10]. The monthly premiums start at 2 Ghana Cedi and may be as high as 10–15 Ghana Cedi if the savings component is chosen[11].

1.3 Theoretical Framework for Insurance Participation

In their pioneering study on participation in an index-based, agricultural micro-insurance, Giné, Townsend and Vickery (2008) present a simple neoclassical benchmark model of households' decisions to take up insurance, which they complement with important insights from behavioral economics. This model has guided the analysis in Cole et al. (2009) and also forms the basis of our theoretical framework. We modify their predictions and add some expectations to match our insurance example and to include insights from standard asymmetric information models on insurance consumption. As noted above, the Anidaso

8 These operate in the same (but formalized) way as so-called "susu" collectors in the informal financial sector, to which we refer below.

9 Financial groups are very common in Ghana. In the formal financial market, they usually have a joint savings account and accumulate savings from their members in order to qualify for a loan. In the case a loan was granted, the group handles the collection of repayments, acts as a mediator between the loan officers and the individual group members, and bears responsibility for recovery. Yet, direct lending to individuals with a credible history as a member of a group or, in cases where a group approach is not suitable, is also common (Steel and Andah 2008).

10 In fact, this feature of the policy is used for promotion purposes in the Anidaso policy information flyer.

11 In our sample of 87 Anidaso policy holders, the mean monthly premium is 3.95 Ghana Cedi and the median is 3.10 Ghana Cedi. The exchange rate at the time of our survey (February 2008) was 1.00 Ghana Cedi = 1.05 US Dollar.

policy is not purely a life insurance, but includes accident and hospitalization benefits. Yet, since we observed that these additional benefits are not as important as the life coverage to policy holders (or are altogether unknown by the policy holders), we treat the Anidaso policy, as if it did not include them at all. In other words, we consider Anidaso a life insurance policy only.

The benchmark model of Giné, Townsend and Vickery (2008) refers to a full information setting and predicts that households' uptake of insurance is increasing in risk aversion, in the expected insurance payout relative to the cost of insurance (in other words, the subjective probability of risk), and in the size of risk exposure (or, the objective probability of risk); and it is decreasing in basis risk, i.e. the correlation between insurance payout and the risk to be insured. Applying the benchmark model to our case, all of these predictions persist with the exception of basis risk, which is not an issue here, as the Anidaso policy is not an index-based insurance. Yet, it is a life insurance, and hence, a bequest motive which is commonly included in standard models of participation in life insurance markets (Yaari 1965, Hakansson 1969, Fischer 1973, Lewis 1989) may be considered. A bequest motive can be expected to increase noticeably when individuals marry or have offspring. Over the lifetime of the consumer, the subjective weighting function for bequests is assumed to take on a hump shape, as the importance of bequests is greatest when the consumer dies at prime age.

It is important to note that the bequest motive is directly applicable only to life insurance that covers mortality risk, generally referred to as term life insurance. The determinants of uptake of permanent life insurance such as whole life insurance, however, may be somewhat different. Hence, some authors take the motive for saving for retirement into account (Pissarides 1980). In practice, many insurance contracts actually serve both bequest and savings motives simultaneously. Empirical evidence has shown that term life insurance and whole life insurance are not necessarily substitute goods, i.e. both motives may coexist (Babbel and Ohtsuka 1989, Outreville 1996).

In principle, the Anidaso policy is a term life insurance as it is pays a determined amount to the insured's family if the insured dies within the policy term. However, due to the (voluntary) savings component, it is not a pure form of term life insurance but may be rather considered a universal life insurance (Black and Skipper 2000). Therefore, insurance participation can be generally expected to be higher when there is a strong motive for a bequest to be left to remaining household members. For those people who choose the savings component, savings motives are likely to play a role as well. It would be plausible to assume a change in preferences over time regarding the utility from expected consumption versus the utility from bequest, i.e. the bequest motive diminishes with increasing age, while the saving-for-retirement motive becomes more important.

Following their benchmark specification, Giné, Townsend and Vickery (2008) augment their simple model with credit constraints so as to account for the fact that the degree of liquidity may play a key role in the decision to participate in insurance. Yet, the relationship between financial constraints and households' willingness to pay for insurance is ambiguous. On one hand, it could be that liquidity-constrained households are more likely to purchase insurance, because they have less ability to deal with the consequences of shocks than households that are not liquidity-constrained. This option was theoretically laid out by Gollier (2003) who explains that self-insurance in the form of reducing savings or borrowing is a substitute to costly formal insurance. He summarizes that "only liquidity constrained households would purchase a generous insurance coverage" (Gollier 2003: 21). On the other hand, in the specific setting of Giné, Townsend and Vickery (2008), insurance is purchased at the same time as agricultural inputs are bought. Hence, credit-constrained households may prefer to use all available funds for inputs, and the authors consider this option more likely than the first. While the Anidaso policy is not directly linked to production decisions, one may still consider the possibility that limited cash would rather be invested in income-generating activities than in insurance to secure (a minimum) future income. In sum, the expected relationship remains ambiguous and the direction of the association would have to be established empirically.

In the light of standard predictions about consumers' insurance-purchasing behavior such as the ones cited here, experiences in the real world have often revealed remaining puzzles. As a potential explanation for insurance participation in developing countries that deviates from the conventional model, Giné, Townsend and Vickery (2008) consider households' trust in the supplier and households' understanding of an insurance policy. Even though the authors do not formally model such behavioral factors, they introduce hypotheses on their relevance for insurance uptake decisions[12]. Specifically, they predict that trust in the vendor, information gleaned from social networks, and greater cognitive ability make insurance purchase more likely. They show that allowing for these

12 Within behavioral finance, trust has often been considered in models of stock market participation. For example, Guiso et al. (2008) show that the perception of risk in stock markets is not only a function of the objective characteristics of the stock, but also of the consumer's subjective probability to be cheated. From a slightly different perspective, Hong et al. (2004) propose that social interaction enhances trust in stock markets in the sense that "social" consumers find it more attractive to invest in stocks when more of their peers participate.

factors helps explain deviations from the benchmark model. Other authors have confirmed the enormous relevance of trust and familiarity with the product and the supplier (Cai et al. 2009, Cole et al. 2009, Thornton et al. 2009), and we expect similar results in our case.

As another potential explanation for observed deviations from the standard model, a number of studies have included adverse selection and moral hazard in models of insurance-purchasing behavior (Rothschild and Stiglitz 1976, Chiappori 2000, Dionne et al. 2000, Winter 2000, Abbring et al. 2003). Different to the case of the rainfall insurance studied by Giné, Townsend and Vickery (2008) and Cole et al. (2009), the life insurance market can be considered a "prime example of a market saddled with the inefficiency associated with adverse selection" (Cawley and Philipson 1999: 827)[13]. Thus, we relax the assumption of full information. In line with asymmetric information models (e.g. Rothschild and Stiglitz 1976), we expect that – given equal premiums and benefits of the policy – households with a higher riskiness (i.e. those with a higher exposure to the insurable risk) tend to purchase the Anidaso policy more than households with a lower riskiness. Since it is rather unlikely that insured households behave less carefully and provoke the risk covered under the insurance (i.e. death), moral hazard, however, is not supposed to present an essential problem.

As noted above, we furthermore assume that there is an association, which may be either positive or negative, between the uptake of microinsurance and the use of other financial services. As we have already outlined, the association is not straightforward: Savings and credit may either be substitutes for microinsurance, or their use may reinforce the uptake of microinsurance. In order to better understand and analyse this matter, it may in fact be necessary to distinguish between savings and loans from formal sources and those from informal sources[14]. In our case, the mutually reinforcing effect of savings and credit on one hand and insurance on the other relates to services provided in the formal financial sector, as the Anidaso policy is solely provided by formal financial institutions. Substitution between savings and insurance as well as between credit and insurance is generally possible for services from both formal and informal institutions. Households may have a precautionary motive in mind, no matter

13 In the analysis of indexed-based insurance by Giné, Townsend,and Vickery (2008) and Cole et al. (2009), information asymmetry does not play a major role because rainfall patterns that are relevant for index-based payouts are public information and rainfall measurement instruments are protected from manipulation by farmers.

14 In the remainder of **Essay 1**, we use the terms formal/informal services and services provided on the formal/informal financial market interchangeably.

whether they deposit their savings in banks or collect them with informal savings groups or at home. In general, loans may be used in order to deal with the consequences of shocks regardless of where they come from. Yet, in reality it may be more difficult to obtain a loan for such a purpose from the formal sector than from social networks, such as extended families. In sum, we expect a negative relationship between the use of informal savings as well as informal loans and the uptake of microinsurance, and a positive relationship between the use of formal loans and microinsurance, while the relationship between formal savings and microinsurance remains inconclusive.

1.4 Sources of Data

The data for our empirical analysis comes from a survey of 350 households in the Central Region of Ghana. Previous studies on households' participation in microinsurance in developing countries have either followed the same approach and used household survey data (Wang and Rosenman 2007, Giné et al. 2008, Ito and Kono 2010) or have conducted randomized experiments (Cai et al. 2009, Cole et al. 2009, Giné and Yang 2009, Thornton et al. 2009). Though the second way of data collection is clearly advantageous in terms of the researchers' control for selection into participation, we could not run such experiments due to time and resource constraints. Nevertheless, we believe that our results allow for external validity, at least to a certain extent, as we explain in the following description of survey sampling.

In a first step, we chose to investigate the Anidaso policy, as GLICO had been identified as the only known insurance provider in sub-Saharan Africa offering voluntary life insurance to low-income households[15]. In a second step, we selected the specific survey area, Brakwa and Benin, from the service areas of all 26 financial institutions that distribute the policy[16]. In doing so, we only con-

15 This selection was done in the year 2007. At that time, all other providers we were aware of had an insufficient number of clients, offered only compulsory (mostly credit life) insurance, or provided health or heavily subsidized agricultural insurance. However, since information on microinsurance providers and products is fragmentary, it may well be that voluntary microinsurance products besides GLICO's Anidaso policy existed that we were not aware of. Due to the dynamic nature of the market, we assume that there are many more voluntary life insurance products today.

16 GLICO has collaborated with the Brakwa RCB since 2005. The bank has its headquarters in the town of Brakwa and a branch office in the district capital Asikuma, which also offers the policy. Both offices are frequented by the population in the survey area.

sidered small to medium-sized towns in semi-urban or rural areas[17], because we intended to make sure that we would find a high share of low-income people in the overall population, assuming that people in rural areas are on average poorer than people in urban areas[18]. We also paid attention to a relatively high density of bank clients holding an insurance contract and to the easy accessibility of the area. Out of five possible survey sites, we randomly chose Brakwa and Benin. Hence, our results should be at least representative for these five semi-urban locations in the South of Ghana where microinsurance is available.

While we acknowledge that external validity is not fully given, we nevertheless believe that the scope for generalization goes beyond the local area of the survey itself. We have little reason to assume that GLICO executes non-random program placement and chooses the cooperating institutions on the basis of particular characteristics. From discussions with GLICO staff, we conclude that in principle the insurer would distribute its microinsurance policy through any formal financial institution that is both interested in doing so and has the ability to deduct the premiums from policy holders' accounts. In the South of Ghana, there are financial institutions (by and large in the form of RCBs or MFIs) in every district capital and also in many other towns that could generally distribute the policy. We acknowledge that there remains some lack of clarity as to why the particular financial institutions were selected to offer Anidaso and not others. Yet, we assume that this selection is simply a matter of the recent emergence of the Anidaso policy and the need to "start somewhere".

Furthermore, Brakwa and Benin are typical towns of the South of Ghana, and the Asikuma/Odoben/Brakwa district in which they are located is an average mostly rural district with a rural population of 68 percent. The district is a highly agrarian, local economy with over 60 percent of the population being engaged in farm activities, mostly at the subsistence level and to a small extent in cash-crop cultivation (for example, cocoa) (Republic of Ghana 2007). Activities outside farming are focused in small-scale industrial businesses and petty trading. We therefore assume that our findings could be replicated in any location in the South of Ghana and similar contexts in sub-Saharan Africa, except for cities and truly remote areas. However, in order to determine to what extent this as-

17 Out of the 26 financial institutions, 11 were located in an urban setting.

18 In 2000, the poverty headcount in the Asikuma/Odoben/Brakwa district amounted to 57.6 percent on average with 42.1 percent in urban areas and 64.8 percent in rural areas. Rural poverty is high in this particular district: The poverty headcount in rural areas in the Central Region as a whole is 46.5 percent. These numbers are based on data from the 2000 census (Coulombe 2008). The IMF (2006) also presents poverty estimates for the district. The poverty headcount is 62 percent in total here, 35 percent in urban areas and 74 percent in rural areas.

sumption is true, further empirical research, including data collection in other locations, is needed.

In Brakwa and Benin, we listed all households and conducted stratified random sampling. We stratified the households according to their insurance membership status. It is important to note that the Anidaso policy is not the only insurance available in the area. Donewell, a commercial insurance company, provides life, accident and car insurance, and there is the public National Health Insurance Scheme (NHIS). The NHIS was launched in 2004 and replaced the cash-and-carry healthcare system[19]. It provides medical care at public hospitals, recognized private hospitals, and health centers for contributors and their dependents. Premiums are graded by income, and particular groups, such as the elderly, indigent people and pregnant women are covered free of charge. The NHIS is well received, particularly in rural areas, where a majority of people had hitherto gone without health services as a result of lacking resources and insurance alternatives.

In our sampling process, the first stratum was formed by households that were not insured at all, the second by households that were insured by the Anidaso policy (and potentially by other insurance as well), and the third by households that were not insured by Anidaso but by other insurance policies. Households within each stratum were chosen through random sampling, except for the microinsured stratum, in which all households were interviewed. The varying sampling probabilities are controlled for by including appropriate weights in the estimations below. A total of 351 households were interviewed, of which 154 were not insured, 87 were Anidaso insured, and 87 were otherwise insured. The survey questionnaire contained detailed sections on demographic and socioeconomic characteristics of the household, household assets, the occurrence of shocks, risk management strategies, household attitudes towards risk, and household financial knowledge. Further, information was gathered on the embedding of households in different financial institutions and the usage of loans, savings products, and insurance. One household did not complete the entire questionnaire, which reduces the number of observations in our analysis to 350 households.

With regard to households' use of credit and savings, we found that households rely on a range of services, both formal and informal. The most frequented formal financial institution is the Brakwa RCB, which offers oppor-

19 The membership in NHIS is legally mandatory (unless alternative private health insurance can be demonstrated). However, in practice it is optional for non-formal sector workers. In 2008, the number of card-holders under NHIS reached 45% of the population (Witter and Garshong 2009).

tunities for savings and loans (and of course the Anidaso policy), on either an individual or a group basis. Another formal institution in the survey area, but much less used, is the Ghana Commercial Bank, which has a branch in Asikuma that offers various types of savings products and loans. The survey data show that at least one MFI and one cooperative are active in the survey area as well. During our field visit, we did not become aware of these and hence do not know their names. We nevertheless include financial services provided by them as formal services in our estimations.

In terms of informal financial institutions, we were able to observe moneylenders, credit groups, and the *susu* system. *Susu* institutions include individual savings collectors, rotating savings and credit associations, and savings and credit "clubs" run by an operator[20]. Furthermore, mutual lending between relatives and other social networks is very common. Eligibility criteria are naturally not defined in these informal activities; however, research has demonstrated that a number of social factors, such as social visibility, reputation and social integration, are of considerable relevance, particularly in order to access informal loans (Ayalew 2003, Fafchamps and Lund 2003, Fafchamps and Gubert 2007, Vanderpuye-Orgle and Barrett 2009, Schindler 2010).

1.5 Definition of Variables

In the below estimations, we distinguish between five categories of financial services that households use. These categories indicate whether or not households used insurance, formal savings options, informal savings options, formal credit, or informal credit in the five pre-survey years. The insurance category is confined to the Anidaso policy[21]. The formal savings category includes savings accounts, current accounts (which are often used for the purpose of savings), and other savings products offered by the formal financial institutions active in the two towns, mainly the Brakwa RCB[22]. Informal savings are savings made within in-

20 In 2003, there were over 4,000 collectors nationwide, collecting the equivalent of an average of US$15 per month from approximately 200,000 clients (Steel and Andah 2008).

21 For robustness checks, we extend the insurance category to also include NHIS insurance and the few other insurance policies available in the area. In our sample, 21 households have some private insurance other than Anidaso and 132 have NHIS. In the total population, the respective shares are 4.68 percent and 26.19 percent.

22 Users of savings options are only those households which can be identified as having intentionally decided to use such a product for the genuine purpose of saving or for safe storage of money. This is important because some households were found to be "pseudo-savers" in the sense that they had opened a savings or current account as a

formal schemes, including within the *susu* system, in self-help groups, and at home. The formal credit category includes all loans taken up from formal institutions. The informal credit category entails loans from informal credit schemes, self-help groups, friends, family members and moneylenders. Of the 350 households analysed, 87 use the Anidaso insurance policy, 168 use formal savings, 175 use informal savings, 84 use formal credit, and 124 use informal credit (Table 1.1)[23]. The use of these services need not be exclusive; on the contrary, many of the households use several of these services simultaneously.

Table 1.1: Use of Financial Services

Services used	Number of households in the sample (total = 350)	Estimated number of households in the survey area (total = 2,042)	Estimated proportion in the survey area (%)
Anidaso policy	87	92	4.51
Formal savings	168	707	34.61
Informal savings	175	1,000	48.97
Formal credit	84	327	16.02
Informal credit	124	732	35.87

Source: Authors' calculation.

Note: Households in the sample are weighted according to their sampling probabilities. Based on the weighted amount of the first column the number of households in the survey area is estimated in the second column. This explains the discrepancy between the proportion of households in the sample and the estimated proportion in the survey area.

Since our analysis primarily aims at examining patterns of insurance uptake, the theoretical framework on insurance participation provides the main guidance for the definition of the explanatory variables to be included. We assume that the determinants of the use of loans and savings options are similar to those of the use of insurance[24]. While this may seem to be an arbitrary assumption at first sight, it actually turns out to be a valid one when looking at the empirical literature on borrowing and savings behavior in developing countries (Deaton

precondition for receiving a loan or purchasing insurance and had since not made use of their account for savings purposes. These households are excluded from the category of savings users.

23 In our sample, 21 households have some private insurance other than Anidaso and 132 have NHIS. In the total population, the respective shares are 4.68 percent and 26.19 percent.

24 This is not to say that the effect of certain determinants is necessarily of the same magnitude and not even of the same sign for credit, savings, and insurance uptake.

1989, 1992, Muradoglu and Taskin 1996, Spio and Groenewald 1996, Pal 2002, Kiiza and Pederson 2002, Jabbar et al. 2002, Pitt and Khandker 2002, Swain 2002, Barslund and Tarp 2008). Where this literature offers additional guidance for the empirical specification, we incorporate relevant variables. We assume here that potential determinants of participation in savings and borrowing may influence the uptake of insurance as well. Table 1.2 provides descriptive statistics for the explanatory variables and Table A. 1 (in Appendix A) summarizes the definition of these[25].

With regard to risk aversion, we use a rough proxy based on the following question in our questionnaire *"How do you see yourself? Are you rather willing or unwilling to take risks?"*. Respondents were asked to rank themselves from "0" (unwilling to take risks) to "5" (willing to take risks). Being aware that this question is rather a measure of risk attitude than of risk aversion, we still use it as a risk aversion proxy as it has been shown to be a good predictor of actual risk-taking behavior (Dohmen et al. 2006). We formed a dummy variable which takes on the value of 1 if the respondent reported a ranking of "4" or "5" in response to the question, i.e. being rather risk loving, and 0 otherwise[26].

We measure size of the insured risk, or the objective probability of risk, with the help of information on the household head's health status. We thereby assume that the head is the main decision-maker in the household who makes decisions on the basis of knowledge about herself. Even though our insurance of interest is not a health but a life insurance, we argue that current health status is related with the probability of death. We formed a dummy variable indicating whether the household head was ill or injured in the past year. We include a second dummy variable which reveals whether the household head received any kind of vaccination.

We consider the subjective probability of risk by an index created through factor analysis[27]. This index is a measure of households' assessments of their own risk situation. It includes information on subjective exposure to illness, ac-

25 In order to avoid potential problems of multicollinearity, we calculated the pairwise correlations between the independent variables as well as the VIFs. We see no reason for concern.

26 We prefer using this binary measure, even though some information of the ordinal structure is neglected, as it minimizes problems arising from individual-specific differences in the use of response scales and as well generates simple and easily interpretable results (Dohmen et al. 2006).

27 The index is created by an factor analysis using principal components factor method. See details on variables included and factor loadings in Table A. 2 (in Appendix A).

cidents and economic shocks, relative to other households in their community[28]. An additional measure for the subjective probability of risk is households' past exposures to shocks, which we control for by including dummy variables on the experience of death, illness and other shocks in the past five years.

In order to consider the relevance of bequest motives, we include age of the household head. Furthermore, we control for the share of dependents in the household and the marriage status of the household head. We included age and age squared because a considerable part of the literature on savings behavior focuses on the savings pattern over a lifetime and hence regards age and age squared as important explanatory factors. The general finding is that the determinants of savings demand in developing countries usually differ from those in developed countries and often contradict the theoretical assumptions of the life-cycle theory or the permanent income hypothesis (Deaton 1992, Muradoglu and Taskin 1996, Spio and Groenewald 1996)[29].

We add a dummy which indicates whether households are in Brakwa or Benin. Earlier studies have pointed out that physical proximity to the providing institution is positively related to the uptake of insurance (Wang and Rosenman 2007). We also control for gender, education and employment status of the household head, assets owned by the household, land usage, and remittance receipt. Most existing studies investigate the association between wealth-related factors (including education) and the use of insurance. Surprisingly, there are several studies that do not find a significant relationship between education and insurance uptake (Wang and Rosenman 2007, Giné et al. 2008, Cole et al. 2009, Ito and Kono 2010). This might be due to the fact that it is not education as such that matters but rather the level of specific knowledge on insurance, or financial literacy in general, which has been found to be significantly related to insurance uptake (Giné et al. 2008). In their study on health insurance uptake, Wang and Rosenman (2007) show that education does matter for a household's perception

---

28 The respective questions in the questionnaire were: "In your opinion is your household more or less exposed to health shocks/road accidents/economic shocks compared to other households in your village?".

29 In short, in terms of the determinants of savings, the permanent income hypothesis differentiates between permanent and transitory components of income. While the first is defined as individual longtime income expectations and consumption over lifetime given the present level of wealth, the latter is the difference between actual and permanent income, which is not normally used for consumption and hence its marginal propensity to be used for savings is unity (Friedman 1957, Kelley and Williamson 1968). The life-cycle hypothesis predicts that individuals smooth their consumption evenly over their lives by accumulating savings during earning years and dissaving after retirement to maintain consumption levels (Ando and Modigliani 1963).

of the need for insurance but not for the final purchase decision. They explain that education relates to the ability of people to assess risk and the way insurance would mitigate it. Yet, whether or not a household finally decides to purchase insurance depends on different factors.

Table 1.2: Descriptive Statistics

Variable	**Mean**	**Stand. error**	**Minimum**	**Maximum**
Willingness to take risk	0.38	0.030	0	1
Illness	0.47	0.029	0	1
Vaccination	0.53	0.030	0	1
Risk assessment	0.07	0.060	-1.158	1.929
Death experience	0.43	0.030	0	1
Illness experience	0.36	0.029	0	1
Other shock experience	0.15	0.021	0	1
Age	47.01	0.941	17	92
Age squared	2,479.54	95.736	289	8464
Share of dependents	0.53	0.017	0	1
Married	0.61	0.030	0	1
Benin	0.20	0.023	0	1
Female head	0.43	0.030	0	1
Schooling	6.51	0.317	0	23
Employee/employer	0.14	0.020	0	1
Assets	-0.17	0.052	-1.196	2.794
Land (ln)	0.55	0.035	0	2.83
Remittances	0.28	0.027	0	1

Source: Authors' illustration.
Note: Households in the sample are weighted according to their sampling probabilities.

Employment status is measured as a dummy variable indicating whether the household head is employed (as opposed to self-employed or not occupied) or an employer. Even though we do not distinguish between formal and informal employment, we suppose that being employed or being an employer is related to more steady income streams. In order to control for potential endogeneity of assets owned by the household, we use the lagged version of an asset index, which captures asset ownership five years ago[30].

The inclusion of employment status as well as land size also follows from our review of the literature on borrowing behavior, while the inclusion of remittance receipt is motivated by the savings literature. With regard to the first, it has been found that investment plans are a much more important driver for the use of formal loans than they are for the use of informal loans. This is reflected in the finding that greater land holdings or area of operational holdings, less wage-labor income, higher price of output and different primary economic activities – factors associated with a higher need for capital in the household – are positively associated with the use of formal loans that are hence geared towards production purposes and asset management (Pal 2002, Swain 2002, Barslund and Tarp 2008). With regard to the latter, it has been found that the receipt of remittances appears to influence the timing of savings within the life-cycle of a household (Spio and Groenewald 1996).

1.6 Estimation Strategy

As in other studies on insurance consumption (Browne 1992, Outreville 1996, Giné et al. 2008), and similar to the literature of public service use (Lavy et al. 1996, Handa 2002, Fafchamps and Minten 2007), for example, our analysis is faced with the problem of limited variance on the supply side. Most studies of this kind therefore rely on reduced-form estimations of households' use of a particular service assuming that use is a function of all arguments in a respective demand and supply function. As a matter of concern, supply side factors may not be (adequately) controlled for. In addition, some variables may simultaneously affect demand and supply and the distinction between them may be blurred for example if it were necessary to be formally employed to open up a savings account and hence also to purchase insurance. In the light of these concerns, we provided very detailed information on the supply of the Anidaso

30 Deviating from the approach in Giné, Townsend and Vickery (2008), we do not control for credit constraints in our estimations. On one hand, this is because our data do not allow for a good measure of credit constraints. On the other hand, the specific empirical model we apply, i.e. estimating the uptake of insurance and the use of credit simultaneously, makes it difficult to include credit-related information on the right-hand side of the estimation equation. Since we include variables for employment status, assets, and land usage, which are different measures of the wealth of a household, they may serve as an indication for credit constraints.

policy and the other financial services above in order to facilitate better interpretation of our results.

In order to investigate the correlates of households' uptake of microinsurance and other financial services, we thus estimate a reduced-form multivariate probit model. Due to the connection to the Gaussian distribution, this allows for flexible modeling of the underlying association structure, i.e. the cross-dependencies in latent utilities across the different services, and straightforward interpretation of the parameters. The alternative choices in the estimation are represented by the five latent variables: use of insurance I^*, use of formal savings options S_1^*, use of informal savings options S_2^*, use of formal loans L_1^*, and use of informal loans L_2^*. Each latent response depends on a vector of explanatory variables X, unknown parameters β_{S1}, β_{S2}, β_{L1}, β_{L2}, β_I, and the stochastic components of the error terms $\varepsilon_{S1}, \varepsilon_{S2}, \varepsilon_{L1}, \varepsilon_{L2}, \varepsilon_I$. The latter consist of those unobservable factors which explain the marginal probability of making the decision for one of the choices. The set of explanatory variables included in vector X is identical in the five equations, assuming that the same decision-making process underlies each choice.

$$
\begin{aligned}
I^* &= X'\beta_I + \varepsilon_I \\
S_1^* &= X'\beta_{S1} + \varepsilon_{S1} \\
S_2^* &= X'\beta_{S2} + \varepsilon_{S2} \\
L_1^* &= X'\beta_{L1} + \varepsilon_{L1} \\
L_2^* &= X'\beta_{L2} + \varepsilon_{L2}
\end{aligned} \quad (1)
$$

The five equations from (1) may be expressed as five binary variables Y_j $(j = I, S_1, S_2, L_1, L_2)$ that take the value of 1 if the household uses a financial service, and 0 otherwise.

$$Y_j = 1(X'\beta_j + \varepsilon_j > 0) \qquad j = I, S_1, S_2, L_1, L_2 \quad (2)$$

Each of these functions can, of course, be estimated as single probit models. However, this would result in inefficient coefficients, if households' choices for financial services are interrelated. Single probit estimations do not allow for a non-zero correlation between the error terms. Therefore, we prefer to estimate a multivariate probit model, in which non-zero correlation is possible and hence provides more efficient estimates (Jones 2007).

In this model, each ε_j is drawn from a J-variate normal distribution with a mean of 0, and a variance-covariance matrix Σ, where Σ has values of 1 on the leading diagonal and correlations $\rho_{jk} = \rho_{kj}$ as off-diagonal elements. These correlation terms represent the unobserved correlation between the stochastic ponent of each type of financial service (Capellari and Jenkins 2003).

The joint estimation of the five alternative equations (2) is based on a joint multivariate probability involving the evaluation of the loglikelihood over I = 1, ..., N observations

$$\ln L = \sum_{i=1}^{N} \ln \Phi_5(\mu_i;\Omega) \quad (3)$$

where $\Phi_5(.)$ is the multivariate normal cumulative density function with arguments μ_i and Ω, where

$$\mu_i = (k_{iS1}\beta_{S1} X'_{iS1}, k_{iS2}\beta_{S2} X'_{iS2}, k_{iL1}\beta_{L1}X'_{iL1}, k_{iL2}\beta_{L2}X'_{iL2}, k_{iI}\beta_I X'_{iI}) \quad (3a)$$

where k_{ij} are the corresponding sign variables that equal 1 if a household uses a given financial service, and -1 otherwise. In matrix Ω, the constituent elements are Ω_{jk}, where

$$\Omega_{jj} = 1 \text{ for } j = 1,\ldots,5 \quad (3b)$$

This function is estimated using the method of simulated maximum likelihood (SML) by application of the Geweke-Hajivassiliou-Keane (GHK) smooth recursive conditioning estimator in order to evaluate the multivariate normal distribution functions (Capellari and Jenkins 2003, Greene 2003). Under the assumption $\varepsilon \sim N(0,\Sigma)$ clarified above, the correlation coefficients summarize the association between unobservable household-specific factors that determine the likelihood of choosing one of the different financial services. The average partial effects (APEs) on the marginal probabilities of the explanatory variables in each equation are estimated by averaging sample partial effects, calculated for each household.

1.7 Estimation Results and Interpretation

The outcome of the multivariate probit regression, showing the APEs of the explanatory variables on the marginal probability to take up any of the five alternatives, is presented in Table 1.3. It is important to note that the outcome categories are not mutually exclusive; in other words, households with an Anidaso policy include those who use Anidaso alone as well as those who use it in addition to any (combination) of the four alternative financial services. The hypothesis that the correlations between the error terms of each equation are jointly zero can be rejected at a high significance level ($X^2 = 6{,}755$; $p = 0.000$); and hence applying the multivariate probit model is appropriate[31].

The estimated correlation coefficients indicate that the residuals of the estimation functions are highly correlated for the formal financial services, indicating that they have very similar unobservable, household-specific determinants. While there is a very strong positive correlation between the use of formal savings and the use of formal credit, the correlation between the uptake of Anidaso and either of the other two formal services is also positive but not as high. The correlation coefficient between the unexplained part of the (simultaneous) use of formal savings and formal loans amounts to 0.98, between Anidaso and formal savings to 0.69, and between Anidaso and formal credit to 0.46. This provides some evidence for a mutually reinforcing relationship between the uptake of formal savings, formal loans, and microinsurance. In terms of the informal financial services, there is a negative correlation between the error terms of the informal credit equation and the insurance equation, and a positive one for the informal savings equation and the insurance equation. This conforms only partially to our expectation of a substitutive relationship between these services and microinsurance. Unobsevered heterogeneity might here explain the positive correlation, as there might be households with lower discount rates which makes them save more and purchase more insurance. However, the correlation coefficients are not statistically significant, thus inhibiting a final conclusion here.

In the following, we mainly interpret the estimation results for the uptake of insurance. We elaborate on the findings for the other financial services only where these appear to be innovative. It is important to note at this point that any inference on causal relationships should be treated with the necessary caution because our analysis is based on cross-sectional data. Thus, we limit our interpretations to associations and do not intend to draw conclusions on causality.

We find that in contrast to the expectations derived from the benchmark model, but in line with Giné, Townsend and Vickery (2008), risk-averse households are significantly less likely to take up microinsurance. This is shown by a comparably large, positive marginal effect of the level of willingness to take risk in the insurance function. In terms of the other financial services, the coef-

31 Note that it would only be appropriate in the case of independent error terms to deal with the above model as independent equations, as explained in the estimation strategy. Nevertheless, we have also estimated the five choice functions as binary probit models (Table A. 3 in Appendix A). With few exceptions, the signs of the estimation coefficients remain the same. Generally, the significance levels are lower in the binary probit compared with the multivariate probit results.

ficients do not exhibit any statistical significance. This suggests that microinsurance is not regarded as a mechanism to mitigate risk but rather as a risky undertaking itself. A rational explanation would be that policy holders do not fully understand the terms and conditions of the insurance, so that they do not trust in that the insurance company is willing to actually pay out the benefit in the case of a claim or is financially stable enough to even exist securing future claims in the long run. A similar finding was shown in Giné and Yang (2009).

In line with this interpretation is the result that households which consider themselves to be more exposed to risk than others are less likely to be Anidaso policy holders. We expected a positive relationship between the subjective exposure to risk and the use of microinsurance. However, it appears that the Anidaso policy is not perceived to be helpful in dealing with risk, at least as far as the risks included in the variable (illness, accident, economic shocks) are concerned[32]. Since we do not know much about causality, it is important to mention that households which do not have access to insurance might be – and feel – more exposed to risk[33]. Regarding the other alternatives, risk assessment is negatively associated with informal savings and positively associated with informal credit, showing larger marginal effects compared with the case of insurance. Since informal loans often serve as ex post coping strategies, this indicates that the risk assessment variable is a good indicator for true risk exposure.

From the predictions of the benchmark model, we expected a positive relationship between the objective size of the risk and the uptake of microinsurance. Indeed, we find a negative association between the vaccination status of the head of the household and the uptake of microinsurance. This might indicate that households with a head who has not received any vaccination tend to purchase the Anidaso policy more than households with a vaccinated head. Since vaccination is very cheap, it is unrational for household heads to not vaccinate and thus endanger their health and the health of the other household members. However, given that vaccination status is not public information and that it is not part of Anidaso's eligibility criteria, this could be an indication for asymmetric information in the market, i.e. potential adverse selection. Yet, we acknowledge that vaccination status is only an imperfect measure of policy

32 We repeated the estimation and substituted risk assessment by only the subjective exposure to health shocks, as this might be the type of risk most relevant for households' decisions to take up the Anidaso policy. This did not change the signs and significance levels of the estimates, except for the fact that the respective coefficient in the formal loan function becomes insignificant.

33 We are grateful to an anonymous referee for pointing this out.

holders' riskiness, and that illness of the household head in the previous year, which is also thought to measure riskiness, is not statistically significant. At the same time, illness of the household head is negatively related to the use of formal credit and positively to the use of informal credit. The marginal effect is particularly large for informal credit. Thus, it seems that households' primary response in the case of the main breadwinner's illness is to borrow from within their social networks.

We find mixed evidence for a bequest motive in the uptake of the Anidaso policy. On one hand, there is no significant relationship between the uptake of insurance and the share of dependents in the household[34] or marriage status of the head. On the other hand, the coefficients for the age variables in the insurance function are of the expected sign and they are statistically significant. They suggest that there is a life-cycle effect in the uptake of the Anidaso policy; whether this life-cycle effect implies a bequest motive, however, is questionable due to the insignificant results of marriage status and share of dependents.

Interestingly, there also seems to be a life-cycle effect for the use of both formal and informal credit. With increasing age of the household head, households request more insurance and more credit, most likely because their experience with financial matters increases, their economic activities are more developed, and their family responsibility increases. Yet, this effect holds only up to a certain age and then reverses. The turning point for uptake of the Anidaso policy is precisely 47 years of age, for formal credit it is 60 years of age, and for informal credit it is 42 years of age. The fact that the turning point for uptake of the Anidaso policy is relatively low suggests that there is no saving-for-retirement motive at play. However, for those households who choose the savings component, the policy might still be seen as a savings instrument, irrespective of a pension. In addition, we find slight evidence for a life-cycle effect in the case of formal savings, which is in contrast to much of the literature on savings behavior in developing countries (Deaton 1992, Muradoglu and Taskin 1996, Spio and Groenewald 1996), but the effect is statistically significant only at the ten percent level.

According to our results, households with more well-educated heads are significantly more likely to purchase the Anidaso policy. This is in contrast to much of the earlier literature, which finds no significant relationship between education and the uptake of insurance (Giné et al. 2008, Cole et al. 2009, Ito and Kono 2010). Our deviating result might be due to the fact that we do not additionally control for financial literacy as many of the mentioned studies do.

34 The results do not change qualitatively when substituting the share of dependents by household size or the share of children in the household.

A higher asset index is positively and significantly related to the use of all formal financial services as well as informal savings, with particularly high marginal effects in the savings equations. This positive relationship is presumably due to the role of assets as collateral for formal loans on one hand and to assets being an indication of the socioeconomic status, and hence of financial literacy and availability of liquid resources for insurance and both formal and informal savings on the other hand[35]. This is in line with the microfinance literature, which shows that microfinance typically does not reach the poorest households (Hulme and Mosley 1997, Navajas et al. 2000, Datta 2004).

Our results suggest that remittances work as a substitute for the Anidaso policy, shown by a negative significant coefficient in the insurance equation, but they are also a source for savings, demonstrated by a positive significant coefficient for the formal savings alternative. Households obviously regard insurance to be less necessary, if they are potentially able to access remittances in cases of future shocks and emergencies.

Residence in Benin is positively and significantly correlated with the uptake of the Anidaso policy (as well as informal savings). Since the bank providing the policy is located in Brakwa, it would have been more plausible to assume that there was a negative relationship due to the relative distance and hence higher transaction costs. However, it seems that the Benin dummy captures information different from pure distance. One possible explanation could be that the PIA, GLICO's main local agent in the area, lives in and is part of the social community of Benin. Hence, trust in the insurance product and the local distributing institution may be enhanced through this personal contact, resulting in a higher likelihood of Benin households purchasing the policy, even though they are farther away from the bank office.

In order to analyse whether these results are specific to the type of microinsurance studied here, we replace the outcome alternative of uptake of the Anidaso policy by uptake of NHIS and uptake of all types of insurance available in the area and repeat the multivariate probit estimations. Table A. 4 (in Appendix A) shows the respective results. We do not illustrate estimates for the financial services other than insurance, as these change only marginally when substituting one insurance category by another. In column (1), we reproduce the results for the Anidaso policy from Table 1.3 to make comparisons easy. In columns (2) and (3), we report the estimates for the NHIS category and the all insurance cate-

35 When running the same regression with the asset index based on current asset levels (i.e. at the time of the survey), the results do not change remarkably. Thus, the potential noise in the regression due to the endogenous nature of assets might actually not be extraordinarily large.

gory of the multivariate probit, respectively. Since the latter category includes all types of insurance available in the sample, including Anidaso, NHIS, and other private insurance policies, the results are likely to be more difficult to interpret. It is not clear to which type of insurance a particular association is to be ascribed, as a positive coefficient resulting from one type of insurance may be cancelled out by a negative coefficient from another type.

As can easily be seen, there are large differences in the estimation results for the Anidaso policy and the NHIS (as well as all insurance policies summarized). Most notably, the relationship between willingness to take risk and uptake of insurance is negative in columns (2) and (3), as the theory suggests, but it is not statistically significant. Hence, the NHIS, and possibly other insurances as well, is neither more preferable for risk-loving households, nor can we say that the likelihood to participate increases for risk-averse households.

Not surprisingly, illness of the household head in the previous year is positively and significantly related with the uptake of the NHIS, showing high marginal effects. The difference between the estimates in the Anidaso function and those in the NHIS function clearly stems from the fact that the former is a life insurance and the latter is a health insurance. It could also be related to the fact that NHIS is subsidized and free for the poorest. Therefore, in contrast to Anidaso, those who are poor and risk averse find it easier to take up NHIS. This, in turn, highlights the suggestion we made above to consider different types of insurance separately.

Similar to the case of the Anidaso policy, there is a strong positive association between residing in Benin and taking up NHIS, and possibly other insurance as well. This points out that the Benin dummy is not merely a measure of trust in the Anidaso policy and the staff distributing it, as the NHIS is not distributed by the same agents. It might instead be a measure of more dynamic interaction within and also between social networks in Benin, as this town is much smaller than Brakwa. The importance of exchange of information within social networks is emphasized in Giné, Townsend, and Vickery (2008). In contrast to the Anidaso policy, the relationship between the receipt of remittances and the purchase of NHIS is positive, indicating that remittances do not always act as substitutes for insurance. The determinants of this relationship remain unclear and seem to be an interesting topic for further research.

Table 1.3: Multivariate Probit Results on the Use of Financial Services

Independent variables	(1) Microinsurance			(2) Formal savings			(3) Informal savings			(4) Formal credit			(5) Informal credit		
	Coeff.	t-stat.	MEs	Coeff.	t-stat.	MEs	Coeff.	t-stat.	MEs	Coeff.	t-stat.	MEs	Coeff.	t-stat.	MEs
Willingness to take risks	0.16	1.13	0.008	0.09	0.47	0.030	0.01	0.03	0.002	0.09	0.45	0.016	0.18	1.01	0.066
Illness	0.24	1.57	0.012	0.05	0.24	0.016	0.12	0.66	0.046	-0.23	-1.09	-0.041	0.34	1.85*	0.121
Vaccination	-0.29	-1.93*	-0.015	0.46	2.54**	0.157	-0.18	-1.01	-0.070	0.56	2.75***	0.099	-0.15	-0.85	-0.055
Risk assessment	-0.09	-1.15	-0.004	-0.01	-0.14	-0.004	-0.23	-2.69***	-0.093	0.01	0.07	0.001	0.18	2.03**	0.065
Death experience	0.11	0.68	0.005	0.28	1.39	0.098	0.36	1.99**	0.143	0.22	0.98	0.039	0.68	3.59***	0.247
Illness experience	-0.02	-0.15	-0.001	0.21	1.05	0.074	0.57	3.04***	0.225	0.46	2.07**	0.090	0.51	2.67***	0.187
Other shock experience	0.08	0.34	0.004	0.29	1.02	0.107	0.04	0.14	0.015	0.93	3.01***	0.239	0.41	1.58	0.157
Age	0.15	3.74***	0.007	0.03	1.03	0.011	-0.07	-2.45**	-0.028	0.09	2.69***	0.016	0.08	2.31**	0.027
Age squared	-0.00	-3.71***	-0.000	-0.00	-0.67	-0.000	0.00	1.98**	0.000	-0.00	-2.42**	-0.000	-0.00	-2.82***	-0.000
Share of dependents	0.04	0.13	0.002	-0.22	-0.68	-0.076	0.82	2.68***	0.326	-0.50	-1.50	-0.090	0.22	0.71	0.080
Married	-0.05	-0.25	-0.002	0.26	1.18	0.090	-0.37	-1.79*	-0.146	0.59	2.69***	0.097	0.24	1.06	0.084
Benin	0.72	4.33***	0.056	0.13	0.59	0.045	0.30	1.54	0.119	-0.18	-0.78	-0.030	-0.09	-0.49	-0.035
Female head	0.07	0.35	0.003	-0.54	-2.34**	-0.183	-0.48	-2.24**	-0.188	-0.09	-0.45	-0.017	-0.04	-0.18	-0.014
Schooling	0.04	2.61***	0.002	0.06	2.97***	0.019	-0.04	-2.00**	-0.014	0.04	1.88*	0.007	-0.04	-1.82*	-0.013
Employee/ employer	0.04	0.17	0.002	0.99	3.68***	0.373	-0.28	-1.13	-0.111	0.50	2.08**	0.111	0.27	1.09	0.101
Assets	0.36	4.67***	0.017	0.29	3.00***	0.104	0.39	3.90***	0.155	0.20	2.07**	0.036	0.04	0.35	0.013
Land (ln)	-0.16	-1.07	-0.008	0.02	0.11	0.006	-0.17	-1.07	-0.066	0.19	1.09	0.033	0.08	0.49	0.027
Remittances	-0.16	-0.89	-0.007	0.49	2.47**	0.177	-0.01	-0.04	-0.003	0.11	0.52	0.021	0.22	1.08	0.080

Source: Authors' calculation.

Note: The model also includes a constant. Sample size is N = 350 observations. Households in the sample are weighted according to their sampling probabilities. The asterisks indicate level of significance: *** significant at 1 percent, ** significant at 5 percent, * significant at 10 percent.

1.8 Conclusion and Scope for Further Research

It is the objective of this paper to contribute to the discussion on the correlates of households' participation in microinsurance in developing countries. Different from previous studies we analyse the example of a micro life insurance. We also deviate from earlier work in our focus on the relationships between households' decisions to take up insurance and to use other financial services. We argue that microinsurance does not enter a vacuum but joins a range of alternative informal and formal financial mechanisms used by households to diversify risk and cope with shocks. We assume that savings and loans could be either substitutes of insurance if they serve a risk management function or their use could reinforce the uptake of insurance if all services are provided by the same financial institution. In order to take into account that households tend to use more than one financial service simultaneously and that there may be interconnections between these, we estimate a multivariate probit model using data from a household survey of 350 households in two neighboring towns in the Central Region of Ghana.

Our estimation results provide evidence for a mutually reinforcing relationship between the uptake of micro life insurance, i.e. the Anidaso policy, and the use of other formal financial services. This is plausible as the Anidaso policy is distributed via local banks, which also offer formal savings options and formal loans. Since we do not know whether this relationship would hold if insurance was supplied and distributed by the insurer itself or via institutions outside the formal financial sector, it would be interesting to repeat our analysis for different provider models and/or in a different context, possibly a different country.

Our evidence does not suggest a substitution, or crowding out, effect between the use of informal savings and informal loans on the one side and uptake of microinsurance on the other side. More precisely, microinsurance does not appear to be simultaneously determined with informal savings or informal loans by the same unobservable, household-specific determinants. This finding is, in fact, not very surprising if we consider that the Anidaso policy covers only the risk of death (and potentially, accident and hospitalization), while households usually face many more risks, such as illness, harvest failure, or unemployment. The policy cannot serve to mitigate all relevant risks; and households simply need to apply other risk management strategies, such as risk sharing within social networks, as well.

In line with earlier studies on households' microinsurance participation behavior, our estimation results reveal certain deviations from a neoclassical benchmark model. We show that risk averse households are less, not more, likely to participate in microinsurance. Furthermore, we find that households which feel more exposed to risk compared to their neighbors are also less likely to participate. Households seem to consider the Anidaso policy to be risky because they do not fully understand the insurance and all its terms and conditions. During our field work, we often got this impression from discussions with the households in our sample. Lack of information on the demand side is generally discussed as one of the most important challenges of microinsurance in academic and policy makers' circles. Our analysis calls this fact into mind again and emphasizes that major efforts are necessary in providing financial literacy to low-income households.

We find indicative evidence for the significant role of trust in the insurance provider and for the role of social networks found in earlier microinsurance studies. Households that live in the smaller one of the two towns in our sample, Benin, which is farer away from the bank office, are surprisingly more likely to purchase the Anidaso policy (and to participate in the NHIS). This is attributed to the fact that there might be a more dynamic interaction within and also between social networks in this smaller town, and that, in the case of the Anidaso policy, the insurer's main local agent lives in and is part of the social community of Benin.

The findings are ambiguous as to the role of a bequest motive, which is usually part of basic life insurance demand models. Our results suggest that there is a life cycle effect in the uptake of microinsurance. Whether this effect is a sign of a bequest motive, however, remains unclear. We furthermore find indicative evidence for adverse selection in the uptake of the Anidaso policy. However, due to suboptimal variables to measure riskiness, we do not want to highlight this very much. We rather hope to see more research on the uptake of micro life insurance using better risk variables in order to investigate the issue of adverse selection further.

Re-estimation of our model taking households' uptake of public health insurance (NHIS) into account reveals that the correlates of health insurance participation differ quite substantially from those of life insurance in general and possibly the Anidaso policy in particular. This stresses the need for additional studies on the uptake of microinsurance, especially with regard to those types of insurance that have not received much attention to date. Having said that, it appears to be desirable to conduct randomized experiments instead of cross-sectional household surveys in further analyses of microinsurance uptake. The main reason for doing so would be to deal with unobserved heterogeneity which might drive some of the results here. The researchers' control over households' selection into participation in randomized experiments allows generalization of findings to a much higher degree.

Essay 2

2. Microfinancial Services and Risk Management: The Perspective from Sri Lanka

Abstract:

This paper examines the importance of financial services as risk coping mechanisms in Sri Lanka. While insurance and savings products function as ex ante, i.e. preventive, strategies for consumption smoothing, credit is typically used as an ex post risk coping strategy. Based on household survey data, this paper estimates the determinants of a household's use of one, two or all three types of microfinancial services by applying ordered probit models and separate probit models for different combinations of financial services. There is empirical evidence that a household's likelihood of participating in microfinancial services increases with its increasing perception of risk. Furthermore, whether a household is more or less likely to use microfinancial services depends, to a large extent, on the type of risk, whereas the accessibility to one, two or three microfinancial services is related to the experience of specific hazards in the past. Following earlier findings, this paper argues that the poor are less likely to use microfinancial services than their better off counterparts in Sri Lanka.

2.1 Introduction

In many developing countries, less than half of the population has access to the formal financial market (World Bank 2008). The lack of access to finance for the majority of the world's population is seen by recent development theorists as a critical way of generating persistent income inequality, as well as revealing slower economic growth. The type of risks faced by the poor, such as those of death, illness, injury and accident, are no different from those faced by the better off, but the poor are clearly more exposed to such risks which can severely affect their livelihoods, due to their economic status, income and earning abilities (Holzmann and Joergensen 2000, Siegel et al. 2001). At two stages a household can cope with risk: ex ante, before a hazard appears to the household, or ex post, after the occurrence of such shock (Morduch 1995, 1999, Townsend 1995, Dercon 2002).

In the past, financial services were not considered to be an option as an ex ante risk management strategy for low-income groups. The poor were seen as too poor to afford the costs of financial services, for instance insurance premiums. Hence, they did not seem applicable for formally provided financial services and even, additionally, were seen as uninsurable for the wide variety of risks they faced. Available evidence for developing countries shows that households are mostly only partially and not fully insured against income shocks (Morduch 1995, Townsend 1995, Lim and Townsend 1998), so that perils to a household's income, such as the death of a household member, often lead to changes in consumption patterns that are not adequately insurable, and which thus might directly or indirectly lead to famine or death. In such cases financial services might serve as means of coping with the present consequences of such (catastrophic) events and by offering savings and insurance products for consumption smoothing to prevent future losses resulting from the occurrence of similar shocks (Zeller 2001). Therefore, the availability of sufficient and efficient risk management strategies are widely considered as an important factor to any poverty reduction strategy.

Microfinance is not only seen as a way to develop the institutional capacities of financial systems by serving the unbanked low-end financial market with loans in an efficient manner, but also a series of measures to combat poverty by improving the financial capabilities of poor households. In recent years the microfinance movement has become more and more demand-oriented and diversified with its introduction of new product lines, i.e. savings and insurance products, to low-income groups in developing countries (Zeller and Sharma 2002, Armendáriz and Morduch 2005). Several contributions in the literature discuss the determinants of households' use of financial services from the microfinance sector in developing countries, focusing primarily on loans, followed, to a lower extent, by savings and insurance (Muradoglu and Taskin 1996, Jabbar et al. 2002, Pal 2002, Swain 2002, Asfaw 2003, Jütting 2003, Bhat and Jain 2006, Barslund and Tarp 2008, Giné et al. 2008). However, none of these assesses the participation in microfinancial services in the context of a more holistic concept of microfinance. To our knowledge, **Essay 1** (Section 1.1) is the first paper to show that households' decisions for taking up loans, savings products and insurance policies are highly interconnected and depend on each other for specific reasons. Taking this into account, we argue here that the microfinancial service participation of low-income households, i.e. the respective usage of zero, one, two or all different types of microfinancial services, gives an indication of the diversification of a household's financial behaviour, in terms of the importance of the risk management strategies in use. By doing so, we assume that the more diversified use of microfinancial services, both in terms of number as well as in quality, i.e. the increasing complexity[36] of the financial services, is determined by the household's level of financial capability.

36 Insurance is widely seen as more complex and thus harder to understand than savings products or loans, especially by the poor.

Therefore, we first attempt to identify the determinants for the three different types of microfinancial services by estimating separate probit models for each financial service. Second, we estimate the determinants which affect the household's decision to use zero, one, two or all three different types of microfinancial services, by using an ordered probit model[37]. In addition, we calculate probit models on specific combinations of financial services, for instance loans and savings. We argue that the estimation of an ordered probit model might add additional value by investigating the kind of factors which determine a household's participation in more than one financial service and whether a higher risk exposure in the past influences the household's decision to diversify and extend the uptake of microfinancial services. From this, we aim to derive insights as to what kind of role microfinancial services might play in terms of risk mitigation. By doing so, it is our objective to contribute to the discussion of the demand and supply side factors determining the participation in microfinancial services offered by MFIs in Sri Lanka. Finally, we identify the households which use more than one service and which use no or only one service; that is, which are the more and which are the less financially capable households.

A comprehensive survey of 330 households conducted in 2008 is used in the analysis. Here, we focus, first of all, on the use of financial services, which is determined by the supply and demand of such services (World Bank 2008). By analyzing the usage of microfinancial services, we do not estimate the determinants of the demand for microfinancial services, but the determinants of their actual use. This use represents a mixture of and interrelation between the demand for and supply of financial services. Only the households who have access to the financial service market can use financial services; thus, we implicitly include such access into our estimation of the usage of such services. We control for the access to financial services by identifying the socioeconomic characteristics of the user and non-user and interpret the result of our estimations concerning the usage of financial services, i.e. the access to financial services on the supply, and especially the demand side.

We find some evidence that households may not link financial service uptake with an additional risk, but it depends on the type of risk whether they can use them as risk coping measures. However, the access to financial services is often limited for them, as it is rather unlikely, considering their high risk exposure in the past and in the future, that the poor would voluntarily choose not to

37 On the one hand unobserved heterogeneity may influence a household's participation in all financial services, but on the other hand a reverse causality may occur, as households without insurance may save more or take up more or higher loans to manage possible future shocks.

use financial services. In addition, there is evidence that household heads with no or little education are more likely to be excluded from the uptake of savings, credit and the combination of savings and credit, which indicates their lack of financial capabilities.

The outline of the paper is as follows. Following this introduction, Section 2.2 presents the conceptual framework of the study. Section 2.3 discusses the determinants of the uptake of financial services in developing countries. A short overview of the microfinance sector and the household's risk exposure in the past in Sri Lanka is presented in Section 2.4. Section 2.5 describes the data, defines the explanatory variables, and discusses the summary statistics. The estimation methodology is presented in Section 2.6 and the results in Section 2.7. Section 2.8 concludes.

2.2 Conceptual Framework

This paper argues that financial services function as important risk management mechanisms; thus, while insurance and savings products are ex ante, i.e. preventive, strategies for consumption smoothing, credit is typically used as an ex post risk coping strategy (Morduch 1995, 1999, Townsend 1995, Dercon 2002). However, a household's choice of loans, savings and insurance products depends on a number of interconnected factors. Such factors include the following (see in more detail **Essay 1**, Section 1.1 and 1.3): First, compared to non-users, users of a financial service have, due to their membership of a financial institution, an informational advantage, and a higher level of financial literacy due to their ongoing experience with financial services while using them. Second, savings play a major role as loan collateral. Third, there are financial products, for instance credit life insurance, which includes a mandatory use of another service. Third, the feasibility and coverage of financial services differs in the case of more diversified hazards. Therefore, we argue that the microfinancial service participation of low-income households, i.e. the usage of no service, one, two or all three types of microfinancial services, gives an indication of the diversification of a household's financial behaviour and the respective risk coping strategies in use.

The study framework structures the relationship between a household's participation in financial services and its level of financial capability, and a household's ability to use these as risk management strategies and its vulnerability[38] (Matul 2009). Covering a wide range of savings, credit and insurance products, financial services are strategies with which to address the specific financial needs of a household. These services can be provided formally or in-informally.

The participation in financial services is also determined by a household's financial capability level, which consists of the knowledge, skills, experience and attitudes which make a household more or less capable of managing its money, preparing for risks, planning ahead and using financial services (PFRC 2005, Matul 2009). Financial capability, or financial literacy as it was initially conceived, is a combination of three interrelated elements, namely the knowledge, skills and attitudes that make a household capable of managing its finances (Rutherford 1999, PFRC 2005, Matul 2009). Financial capability is a relative, not an absolute concept (Rutherford 1999, PFRC 2005). It may be possible to define a basic level of financial capability that is required by everyone in a given society (PFRC 2005). Beyond that, the degree and nature of financial capability required by any given individual will be determined by their financial circumstances (PFRC 2005). This knowledge is acquired by experience, education and training; and passively through information from various other sources, e.g. family and friends, media, brochures from, and information meetings organized by, MFIs. The state of knowledge will typically increase throughout a person's life, but it can become redundant or inaccurate if circumstances change (PFRC 2005). The person's knowledge needs to be applicable to managing their money and to make appropriate financial decisions. People must be able to take the necessary steps to apply their knowledge and skills, which depends highly on their attitude towards financial capability. They must be willing to invest time and other resources in order to apply their knowledge and skills, to be able to gain access to information, advice and other resources, and to be confident enough to exercise their skills and to act on the results.

In behavioural terms[39], our analysis differentiates between more or less financially capable households (Matul 2009). On the one hand, a more financially capable household is proactive, has a positive attitude towards managing its finances, envisions longer horizons in financial planning, saves systematically, tries to insure or at least prepare for risks, and borrows in a responsible way

38 Vulnerability is defined here as a combination of a household's risk exposure and its ability to manage such risks, the related consequences, and the participation in microfinancial services as measures for managing shocks (Siegel et al. 2001, Cohen and Sebstad 2003, Matul 2009).

39 Four different areas of financial capability are identified, which are money management, planning ahead, risk preparation and usage of financial services (PFRC 2005).

(PFRC 2005, Matul 2009). Hence, the household uses differentiated financial services, i.e. more than one service, which may lead to higher asset accumulation in the future. On the other hand, a less financially capable household is more reactive, does not see much sense in using financial services or is not able to manage money, or plan ahead, and tends to live from hand to mouth and respond spontaneously to risks (PFRC 2005, Matul 2009). The household typically uses fewer financial services than the more financially capable household. This leads to a lower ability to respond to risks which might occur in the future and thus to a higher level of vulnerability. We analyse which are the more and which are the less financially capable households, i.e. we consider the determining household characteristics.

Financial capability is highly related to a household's vulnerability (Matul 2009). The degree of a household's vulnerability depends on the characteristics of the risk and especially the household's ability to adequately address the expenditures which are associated with the consequences of such risks[40]. Vulnerability can be divided into three steps of a risk chain: the incidence of the risk or risky event, the household's decision to choose which type of risk management strategy is feasible as an appropriate response to the consequences of the peril, and finally what is the outcome, i.e. the welfare loss of the household, due to the incidence of the risky event (Siegel et al. 2001). If the household's welfare decreases after the experience of the shock, its vulnerability therefore comes explicitly from risks; moreover, the relative impact of risks shows the degree of such vulnerability.

2.3 Determinants of the Uptake of Financial Services

Building on its financial capability, we analyse the household's participation in financial services, as a possible strategy for managing the risks they face. Therefore, it is important to note that there are several empirical findings in the literature on the determinants of the usage of financial services in developing countries, from which we derive predictions to control for in the estimations. The literature can be divided into three strands, each separately analysing one service of the three elements of the finance trinity (**Essay 1**, Section 1.3). There are considerably more studies which focus (particularly) on the issue of credit (Atieno 1997, Kochar 1997, Jabbar et al. 2002, Nguyen et al. 2002, Pal 2002, Pitt and Khandker 2002, Swain 2002, Zeller and Sharma 2002, Barslund and

40 "A household can be vulnerable to future loss of welfare below socially accepted norms caused by risky events." (Siegel et al. 2001: 4).

Tarp 2008) than on savings (Gupta 1970, Deaton 1992, Gurgand et al. 1994, Muradoglu and Taskin 1996, Spio and Groenewald 1996, Fafchamps et al. 1998, Kimuyu 1999, Aryeteey and Udry 2000, Kiiza and Pederson 2002, Hoogeven 2003) or on insurance in developing countries (Asfaw 2003, Jütting 2003, Cohen et al. 2005, Bhat and Jain 2006, McCord et al. 2006, Giné et al. 2008, Cole et al. 2009, Giné and Yang 2009). None of these studies estimate the differences between the determinants of a household's participation in zero, one, two or three microfinancial services. Nevertheless, all studies consider the impact of different determinants, especially several demographic and socioeconomic household characteristics, on financial service uptake, determinants which are of particular importance for our analysis.

In the literature, female-headship is viewed as being negatively related to the use of financial services (Pitt and Khandker 2002). Several contributions recognized household size as an important determinant of the use of financial services (Swain 2002, Dror et al. 2007, Barslund and Tarp 2008). Furthermore, there is evidence of a negative relation between age and the demand for informal credit (Barslund and Tarp 2008) and for insurance (Chankova et al. 2008, Giné et al. 2008). **Essay 1** (Section 1.7) reveals such a life-cycle effect for the participation in loans and insurance schemes in Ghana. Several contributions have found that the household is more likely to take up financial services, especially loans (Kiiza and Pederson 2002, Pal 2002, Pitt and Khandker 2002) or contract insurance, with the increasing income or wealth of the household (Jütting 2003, Pauly 2004, Bhat and Jain 2006, Dror et al. 2007, Giné et al. 2008). Higher asset endowment and land ownership of a household is generally expected to have a positive effect on the choice of taking up one or more financial services, whereas it is expected that lower income earning abilities due to low-scale self-employment or unemployment are negatively associated with the use of financial services. The fact that a household receives remittances can influence the timing of savings within the life-cycle of a household (Spio and Groenewald 1996) and increases the likelihood for the uptake of savings products while decreasing it for insurance uptake, which underlies its savings' function as an insurance substitute (**Essay 1**, Section 1.7).

Education is a significant determinant for credit (Jabbar et al. 2002, Pitt and Khandker 2002, Swain 2002, Barslund and Tarp 2008), savings (Kiiza and Pederson 2002) and for insurance uptake (Chankova et al. 2008, Giné et al. 2008, McCord 2001). Households differ in their cognitive ability to understand an insurance product and other financial services as well as their willingness to experiment with them. Hence, we argue, in line with the literature, that lower levels of educational attainment reduce the probability of using any of the three financial services. The positive effect of education is expected to be particularly strong for the use of more than one service or of insurance, as this goes along with more sophisticated participation in financial services, a better understanding of complex financial services and a higher level of the household's financial capability.

In developing countries, loan schemes play a significant role in the risk management of a household, i.e. the use of credit not only to start a new business activity, but also in the form of additional working capital or to restart a business after recovery from a shock (Zeller and Sharma 2002, Nguyen et al. 2002). A positive relationship exists between a household's past exposure to shocks and the use of various microfinancial services for the tested risks such as death or illness (**Essay 1**, Section 1.7). Therefore, we propose that households with a higher exposure to risks are more likely to use loans, but less likely to use savings and insurance after a shock. We expect a complex picture for the wide variety of the risks we control for.

Giné et al. (2008) find that risk averse low-income households do not have access to insurance, whereas households which feel themselves more exposed to risk are less likely to use financial services (**Essay 1**, Section 1.7). It is plausible to argue that better off households have a better ability and willingness to bear a given amount of risk compared to relatively poor households, so that the poor are most risk averse in developing countries. They are too close to subsistence, so that a given loss can be ruinous for them (Ray 1999). Therefore, we suggest that the use of financial services by low-income households increases with the degree of risk aversion in Sri Lanka.

2.4 Microfinance Sector and Risk Exposure in Sri Lanka

In Sri Lanka, the main providers of microfinancial services consist of co-operatives, Non-Governmental Organisations (NGOs), Community-Based Organisations (CBOs) and the Government's Samurudhi Savings and Credit Programme. The MFIs have a broad coverage, except for in the Northern and Eastern regions (Gant et.al 2004). Sri Lanka has a rapidly growing emerging microfinance market; indeed it has the fourth highest ratio of borrowing clients to total population among the 20 countries with the highest microfinance penetration in the world (World Bank 2008). Even though Sri Lanka has one of the most diversified microfinance sectors in the South Asian region, the ultimate users of microfinancial services are mainly households in the middle quintiles (Tilakaratna et al. 2005).

We asked the households surveyed to list the most important, second most important and third most important sources of future risks in the forthcoming five years. By doing so, we aimed to identify the risk exposure of the household and the risks with the highest impact on the household's income and consumption in the future. In Table 2.1, sources of risks based on self reported rankings are presented from the survey data, which are used later on as determinants in the analysis according to their importance. The households report war and terrorism (19%) as the most important peril they face in the future; a dramatic increase of input prices (18%) and serious illness of a working adult household member (8%) are cited second and third most frequently. Environmental or weather related shocks such as drought (8%) or floods (1%) and economic shocks, for instance the loss of their job (5%), follow with significantly lower frequency. Other important family related shocks such as death or disablement of a working adult or other household member are reported only in a minor proportion of the households.

Overall, there is evidence that family related shocks are key risks faced by households, while a relatively high share cites the impact of war and terrorism, which are associated with individual harm, and the serious illness of a working adult household member as important risks they face in the future. The death of a household member is rarely reported, indicating its lower importance for the households. Nevertheless, in terms of severity the death or severe illness of any household member, or an accident or illness leading to permanent disability are generally seen by respondents as those risks that have the highest financial impact on the household's income and consumption.

Family related shocks are generally characterised by their low frequency, so that they are suitable for a microinsurance scheme. Risks with higher frequency and impact such as less serious health problems are harder to insure as they are predictable and recurrent events. Aggregate or covariate shocks such as weather related risks like drought or flood, and economic shocks, for instance the dramatic increase of input prices, are harder to insure or and the insurance can only be limited for these due to their covariate nature (Townsend 1995). Therefore, the provision of credit, as a form of ex post risk management, or of any savings product, as an ex ante risk coping mechanism, might play a key role for low-income households in coping with the consequences of the risk they face and in sufficiently smoothing income and consumption.

Table 2.1: Sources of Risk in Sri Lanka

What are the major risks that you face?				
Sri Lanka	**Frequency**			**Weighted sum**
	1st reason	**2nd reason**	**3rd reason**	
War/terrorism	70	20	18	19.06%
Increase in input prices	61	27	10	17.57%
Serious illness of working adult household member	29	13	5	8.39%
Drought	21	19	11	7.97%
Loss of job	18	5	11	5.33%
Forced contributions /arbitrary taxation	15	8	5	4.69%
Animal threats	11	12	7	4.55%
Tidal waves	9	9	4	3.49%
Hurricanes	8	6	7	3.06%
Serious illness of other household member	9	5	5	2.99%
Family disputes	6	5	2	2.13%
Crop failure	4	4	9	2.06%
Landslides	6	3	3	1.92%
Inability to sell agricultural products	0	9	9	1.92%
Decrease in output prices	1	6	11	1.85%
Floods	4	3	2	1.42%
Inability to sell non-agricultural products	1	7	3	1.42%
Destruction/theft other assets	2	5	2	1.28%
Marriage	4	3	0	1.28%
Destruction of house	4	0	3	1.07%
Theft of cash	2	4	1	1.07%
Political discrimination	0	6	1	0.92%
Death of working adult household member	3	1	1	0.85%
Childbirth	2	2	1	0.78%
Ethnic/social discrimination	2	1	3	0.78%
Fire	3	0	0	0.64%
Theft of crops/livestock	1	2	0	0.50%
Disablement of working household member	1	1	1	0.43%
Death of other household member	1	0	0	0.21%
Resettlement/Forced migration	1	0	0	0.21%
Disablement of other household member	0	1	0	0.14%
Total	299	187	135	100%

Source: Authors' calculation.

Note: Responses are classified into the categories listed above. The "weighted sum" percentage is the sum across all three categories where 1st, 2nd and 3rd most important reasons are given weights of 1, 2/3 and 1/3 respectively.

2.5 Sources of Data and Summary Statistics

The analysis of this paper is based on a household survey conducted from May to July 2008 all over Sri Lanka. The survey was undertaken for a research project on the demand for microinsurance among low-income households in Sri Lanka. In total, 330 households were interviewed, including two strata of (micro)insured and non-insured households where the latter functioned as the control group.

For the insured strata, we chose five different MFIs, namely the Women's Development Federation (WDF), the Women's Development Banking Federation (WDBF), Sanasa Insurance Company (SANASA), Yasiru Mutual Fund (YASIRU) and SEEDS (Sarvodaya Economic Enterprises development services Ltd) as the main providers of voluntary[41] microinsurance for low-income households in Sri Lanka. These providers offer various insurance types, such as health, life, other life-cycle event, vehicle insurance, old age annuities/pension, credit, crop, and property insurance.

The survey outreach covered all provinces, that is, it included 14 districts in which these MFIs operate. From each district, two or three MFIs were selected, except from the districts of Vavuniya and Batticaloa. These are located in the Northern and Eastern provinces where only one of the selected MFIs, namely SEEDS, is operating. The selected number of insured and non-insured households from each district varies from 15 to 50.

The client bases of these institutions were used to select the insured clients. A selected number of households from each institution were randomly allocated across the districts in which they operate. Villages were selected in consultation with the district branch manager and staff, so that two or three villages were selected from each district, these representing the respective MFIs from the district. By doing so, we ensured that a high share of insured households were easily accessible for the survey. In total, 30 villages were covered under this study, including 10 to 15 insured and non-insured households. However, we suggest that our findings are (at least) representative for villages all over Sri Lanka in which microinsurance is accessible via the selected MFIs. We therefore argue that our results might be replicable in any villages of a rural and semi-urban nature in Sri Lanka, beside large cities, or very remote areas without

41 The participating institutions provide credit insurance policies as well, which are compulsory for the uptake of a loan or other financial product. However, these forms of credit insurance are not considered in this study and the respective observations have been dropped from the data set.

any access to microfinance. We assume that the generalisation goes beyond the survey areas, even though external validity is not fully valid.

As YASIRU and SANASA, two of the covered MFIs, are exclusive insurance providers, we chose the non-insured clients not from the client base of the MFIs directly, but from a list of households received from existing CBOs, which are not linked to the respective MFIs, in the villages[42]. The non-insured clients were randomly selected from households of one CBO in each village. This CBO was picked randomly from a list of existing CBOs in each village, created with the help of the branch manager and the staff members of the MFIs in the district.

Therefore, the total number of households – both insured and non-insured – selected from the villages linked to one of the five institutions varies from 40 to 95 depending on the number of districts in which the MFIs operate; thus, only 40 clients were linked to the WDF, which operates in one district (i.e. Hambantota), while 95 clients were associated with SEEDS, which operates in all the districts in the country. 65 clients were related to each one of the other three institutions (i.e. WDF, WDBF and SANASA).

The sampling was done using two strata of households: those that were insured by one of the covered MFIs and those that were not insured at all. Out of the 330 households, 240 households bought and 90 did not purchase any microinsurance. Furthermore, 209 households have taken up a loan and 200 contracted a form of savings product in the past five years; thus, they might be linked to an MFI for a reason other than insurance. We include appropriate weights in the estimations to control for different sampling probabilities.

The survey questionnaire contained detailed sections on demographic and socioeconomic household characteristics, household assets, the occurrence of shocks, risk management strategies, evaluation of household's risk self-assessment and risk situation. Special focus is given on information about the integration of households into the financial market, and the use of loans, savings products and, in particular, insurance. All analyses were performed in Intercooled Stata 9.0. In the estimations the vector of explanatory[43] variables includes a household's self perception towards risk index expressed as a con-

42 We did so due to limited financial resources for the survey.

43 Table B. 1 (in Appendix B) shows the definition and specific details of each variable's construction, considered as an independent variable. To test for potential problems of multicollinearity, we computed the pairwise correlations between the explanatory variables; for the correlation matrix of the explanatory variables, see Table B. 3 (in Appendix B). We calculated the VIFs using the *collin* command in Stata. Except for the regressors "age" and "age squared" all VIFs were less than 2.21. Therefore, we see no reason for concern regarding multicollinearity.

tinuous variable, eight risk exposure dummies, and as control variables different household characteristics including demographic and wealth variables, education, economic activities of the household head, the distance to road as an access to market indicator and information about remittances.

In relation to the dependent variables, summary statistics for the sample are presented, divided into the mean of each explanatory variable. Table 2.2 displays the summary statistics for the full sample, and the users of savings products, loans, and insurance. In Table 2.3 the descriptive statistics are presented in relation to the categories of the dependent variable used in the estimations of the ordered probit model, namely non-users of microfinancial services, and users of one, two or three microfinancial services.

In order to capture a household's attitude towards risk as a proxy for its degree of risk aversion, we created an index using a factor analysis which covers the household's subjective perception of its exposure to a range of risks[44]. The index is constructed from three questions related to the household's self-perception of its exposure to health shocks, weather and environmental related shocks, and economic shocks, as compared with neighbouring households and from one question about the household's own rating of its willingness to take risks[45]. The users of a loan or savings product report higher risk assessment scores than all households (in the full sample). The users of insurance give themselves the lowest risk assessment score. In addition, the non-users report the highest score for risk assessment, followed, in order, by the users of three, two and one services. In relation to the risk exposure experienced by the household in the past five years, we control for eight different dummy variables in our analysis. These variables capture the most severe risks that households faced in Sri Lanka in the past five years. The variable takes the value of 1 if a household had experienced a severe shock during the previous five years and this had severe consequences, and 0 otherwise. Severity is defined as meaning that the household needed more than one month to recover economically from the specific shock. The dummy variables are if a household experienced a severe drought, animal threat, crop failure, death of a household member, illness of a household member, an increase of input prices, the inability to sell agricultural products, or any other severe shock during the preceding five years. This cate-

44 The index is created by a factor analysis using the principal components factor method. For details on variables included and factor loadings (Table B. 2 in Appendix B).

45 We cannot take risk aversion into account in our analysis, as e.g. are suggested by Dohmen et al. (2006) in the literature on insurance demand, since experimental methods used to measure personal risk aversion were not included in our survey and related standardized questions in our survey questionnaire only reflect this in a limited way.

gory captures mostly idiosyncratic shocks, which may occur in addition to hazards already covered by the other seven risk categories.

Table 2.2: Summary Statistics: Full Sample and Separate Use of Savings Products, Loans and Insurance

Variable	Full Sample		No Service		Savings		Loans		Insurance	
	Mean	Std. error	Mean	Std. Error	Mean	Std. error	Mean	Std. error	Mean	Std. error
Household's self-perception of risk	9.9e-09	0.168	0.146	0.309	0.019	0.078	0.036	0.083	-0.0003	0.069
Drought	0.116	0.016	0.057	0.041	0.106	0.020	0.119	0.021	0.118	0.018
Animal threat	0.078	0.015	0.026	0.026	0.082	0.019	0.078	0.019	0.079	0.016
Crop failure	0.070	0.015	0.031	0.031	0.083	0.021	0.087	0.021	0.070	0.017
Death experience	0.073	0.014	-	-	0.079	0.021	0.081	0.021	0.072	0.017
Illness experience	0.142	0.019	0.152	0.077	0.169	0.028	0.153	0.025	0.145	0.022
Input	0.185	0.023	0.094	0.444	0.209	0.032	0.213	0.030	0.191	0.025
No ability to sell agricultural products	0.089	0.017	-	-	0.101	0.023	0.105	0.023	0.095	0.019
Other risk experience	0.077	0.015	0.072	0.031	0.087	0.022	0.084	0.019	0.074	0.017
Female head	0.169	0.021	0.146	0.082	0.148	0.027	0.161	0.027	0.154	0.024
Household size	4.094	0.078	3.906	0.228	4.129	0.101	4.242	0.099	4.149	0.086
Age	47.88	0.674	50.47	2.345	48.02	0.839	47.63	0.831	47.31	0.729
Age squared	2428.7	64.5	2669.1	240.95	2428.9	84.14	2395.9	81.69	2367.0	71.52
No or only primary education	0.191	0.021	0.272	0.093	0.163	0.028	0.192	0.028	0.166	0.024
Secondary education	0.409	0.027	0.467	0.107	0.355	0.035	0.384	0.036	0.373	0.031
Head is self-employed	0.594	0.027	0.614	0.106	0.571	0.037	0.564	0.037	0.568	0.032
Head is unemployed	0.221	0.023	0.272	0.093	0.199	0.031	0.234	0.032	0.220	0.027
Distance to road	316.14	44.70	721.14	241.11	266.83	47.43	190.14	24.04	303.60	48.01
Remittance	0.051	0.014	0.031	0.031	0.048	0.017	0.060	0.018	0.052	0.015
Land ownership	0.773	0.023	0.516	0.104	0.854	0.027	0.819	0.028	0.812	0.026
Asset index	-1.9e-09	0.055	-0.863	0.125	0.283	0.066	0.123	0.073	0.143	0.062
Observations	330		26		200		209		240	

Source: Authors' calculation.

The summary statistics produce a similar result for the users of savings products, loans, or insurance, due to the exposure to the respective eight risk dummies. The risk exposure of the three user groups depends significantly on the type of risk. In addition to the variables, such as illness of a household member or any other severe shock, a higher share of the users of one, two or three financial services report the incidence of a severe shock than do non-users of financial services.

An asset index constructed via factor analysis and a dummy variable for land ownership are used as proxies for the wealth status of the household. Furthermore, we added asset quintile dummies in one estimation to examine the households which used any kind of financial service, in relation to their wealth status. We checked whether any financial services, such as construction loans, are used to purchase any form of asset; if so, these assets are not considered in the asset index. By doing so, we avoid potential problems of endogeneity. Land is generally not an as easily purchasable asset compared to other assets, so the influence of endogeneity can be neglected. A higher share of the users of savings products, loans or insurance own land compared to those in the full sample. The same is true for the users of one, two or three financial services as compared to the non-users of financial services. The users of three financial services have the highest asset endowment, followed by the users of two and then one financial service. The non-users present the lowest asset endowment score. The users of financial services are generally better off households than the non-users in the communities surveyed. The data set in general, but especially the demographic and wealth data, confirms that the sample consists of poor and middle-income households.

The majority of households is engaged in low-income economic activities such as small-scale industrial businesses, petty trading and farm activities at the subsistence level. Around 20 percent of household heads have no formal or only primary education, whereas 40 percent of households heads report that they received secondary education. Around 60 percent of the household heads are self-employed or contractual workers in either agriculture or non-agricultural activities, while around 20 percent of heads are not employed, due to youth or old age, disability, or similar reasons. The influence of the household size on the usage of financial services depends significantly on the composition of the households. In our data set, household size correlates highly with the number of dependents (correlation coefficient of 0.79) and with the number of children (correlation coefficient of 0.49).

Table 2.3: Summary Statistics: Use of Zero, One, Two or Three Microfinancial Services

Variable	No Service		One		Two		Three	
	Mean	Std. Error	Mean	Std. error	Mean	Std. error	Mean	Std. error
Household's self-perception of risk	0.146	0.309	-0.246	0.066	-0.006	0.114	0.061	0.100
Drought	0.057	0.041	0.146	0.043	0.109	0.025	0.115	0.027
Animal threat	0.026	0.026	0.097	0.039	0.066	0.021	0.087	0.026
Crop failure	0.031	0.031	0.041	0.027	0.051	0.018	0.102	0.029
Death experience	-	-	0.044	0.035	0.075	0.025	0.082	0.027
Illness experience	0.152	0.077	0.063	0.037	0.121	0.028	0.187	0.037
Input	0.094	0.444	0.197	0.049	0.095	0.024	0.275	0.044
No ability to sell agricultural products	-	-	0.080	0.038	0.058	0.021	0.129	0.033
Other risk experience	0.072	0.031	0.055	0.023	0.072	0.023	0.089	0.028
Female head	0.146	0.082	0.191	0.049	0.147	0.033	0.155	0.036
Household size	3.906	0.228	3.750	0.202	4.034	0.113	4.310	0.135
Age	50.47	2.345	45.47	1.832	46.88	1.007	48.337	1.096
Age squared	2669.1	240.95	2233.3	171.16	2317.2	98.17	2461.9	109.51
No or only primary educ.	0.272	0.093	0.162	0.049	0.153	0.032	0.188	0.038
Secondary education	0.467	0.107	0.415	0.067	0.376	0.045	0.363	0.046
Head is self-employed	0.614	0.106	0.633	0.059	0.571	0.046	0.558	0.048
Head is unemployed	0.272	0.093	0.248	0.063	0.179	0.036	0.241	0.043
Distance to road	721.14	241.11	664.64	149.25	307.86	69.91	180.05	27.89
Remittance	0.031	0.031	0.072	0.039	0.027	0.014	0.069	0.025
Land ownership	0.516	0.104	0.665	0.060	0.748	0.041	0.895	0.030
Asset index	-0.863	0.125	0.053	0.129	-0.069	0.092	0.353	0.088
Observations	26		67		129		108	

Source: Authors' calculation.

However, larger households in the sample have a high number of children and elderly people, but also more economically active adult household members. On average, we find that households who use savings products, loans, or insurance, have a larger household size compared to the full sample. Moreover, households who use two or three financial services have larger households than non-users of financial services, whereas users of savings products have the smallest households. The age of the household head shows no large difference between users in the full sample, and the users of savings products, loans or insurance, but the non-users of financial services are significantly older than the users of one, two, or three financial services.

2.6 Methods

The participation in the three formal financial service alternatives – savings products, loans, and insurance – is estimated in the form of separate probit models for each of the three. The analysis is complemented by estimating an ordered probit model on a number of alternatives: whether households used financial services or not, and if so, one, two or all three, in the previous five years. Financial services are defined here as services provided by a state, development, domestic private, or foreign private bank, MFI, insurance company or financial leasing company.

Formal savings products include all formal financial services, which are voluntarily used for a savings purpose, for instance savings accounts, current accounts or savings plans[46]. We control for that by excluding all savings products, which were compulsory or bound to any other formal financial service, so that users of formal savings products are only those households which use these products for the genuine purpose of the saving or safe storage of money. Formal loans include all loans taken up voluntarily from the mentioned institutions and which were not used for the purchase of any durable assets in the previous five years. Formal insurance is confined to those types of insurance which are offered by the MFIs or other insurance providers covered by the survey conducted, and which may be understood as private suppliers (Table 2.4).

Table 2.4: Number of Insured Households Associated with Insurance Providing MFI

Use of insurance provided by	Number of insured households in the sample
WDF	29
WDBF	48
SANASA	51
YASIRU	47
SEEDS	65
Total	240

Source: Authors' illustration

Hence, the category includes mainly health and life insurances, but also many other types of insurances, such as other life cycle events, vehicle insurance, old age annuities/pension, credit[47], crop and property insurance.

46 The related questions in the survey's questionnaire only mentioned savings and do not ask about or distinguish between any specific savings products.

47 Credit (life) insurance policies are not taken into account in this study, as these policies are mostly not taken up voluntarily, but bound to a loan or to the approval of a loan.

The usage of savings products S^*, usage of loans L^*, and usage of insurance I^* is estimated separately using probit models:

$$S^* = X'\beta_S + \varepsilon_S \qquad (1)$$
$$L^* = X'\beta_L + \varepsilon_L$$
$$I^* = X'\beta_I + \varepsilon_I$$

In each of the three equations, each latent variable depends on a vector of explanatory variables X, three unknown parameters β_S, β_L, β_I, and the stochastic components of the error terms ε_S, ε_L, ε_I. The latter represent the unobserved factors, i.e. the marginal probability, accounted for making the decision in favour of either of the three financial services. The dependent variables are the dummy variables below; participation in savings products, loans and insurance (Table 2.5). The vector X of explanatory variables is identical in all three equations and in the ordered probit estimation, assuming that the same decision making process underlies each choice. The three equations from (1) may then be expressed as three binary variables Y_j $(j = S, L, I)$ that take the value of 1 if the household uses a financial service, and 0 otherwise.

$$Yj = 1(X'\beta j + \varepsilon j > 0) \qquad j = S, L, I \qquad (2)$$

Table 2.5: Definition of Dependent Variables

Variable	Description
Use of savings	Dummy variable, 1 if household uses savings, 0 otherwise.
Use of loans	Dummy variable, 1 if household uses a loan, 0 otherwise.
Use of insurance	Dummy variable, 1 if household uses insurance, 0 otherwise.
Use of financial service	Categorical dependent variable for the ordered probit model. 1 if household does not use any financial service, 2 if household uses one financial service, 3 if household uses two financial services, 4 if household uses three financial services (Ordered Probit).

Source: Authors' illustration.

Table 2.6 and Table 2.7 show that the use of each of these services may be interrelated, as many of the households use several of these services simultaneously. Therefore, the estimation results of the separate probit models are combined first with probit models to estimate the determinants of the use of specific combinations of financial services[48] and then with the estimation of an

48 The specific combinations of financial services, such as the use of insurance and loans or savings and loans, which are estimated here with separate probit models, are not totally independent from each other, so the usage is not exclusive. Even though a

ordered probit model with a categorical dependent variable, which has the value one for "no financial service", two for "one financial service", three for "two financial services" and four for "all three financial services". The outcomes are here ordered in relation to the quantity of financial services used by the household. Nevertheless, these quantitative measures indicate important qualitative implications. From the first category use of "no financial services" to the latest category use of "all three financial services", not only the quantity, but also the sophistication and complexity of the use of financial services gradually increases.

Table 2.6: Use of Savings Products, Loans and/or Insurance

Use of	Number of households in the sample
None	26
Savings only	23
Credit only	16
Insurance only	28
Savings and credit	133
Savings and insurance	152
Credit and insurance	168
Savings, credit, and insurance	108
Total	330

Source: Authors' illustration

Table 2.7: Use of Zero, One, Two or Three Financial Services

Use of	Number of households in the sample
None	26
One financial service	67
Two financial services	129
Three financial services	108
Total	330

Source: Authors' illustration

The ordered probability model is a suitable tool for this kind of dependent variable (Greene 2003). The two alternative model types are the ordered logit and the ordered probit model, from which we chose to employ the ordered probit model. The logit specification is only a trivial modification and appears to

multinomial logit model would be a very interesting approach, it is not feasible for these categories, as we cannot assure exclusive categories here.

make virtually no difference in practice (Greene 2003). The ordered probit model is built around a latent regression in the same manner as the binomial probit models and based on the following specification:

$$y^* = \beta' x + \varepsilon. \tag{3}$$

Where x is the vector of explanatory variables set and ε is the disturbance term. As usual y^* is unobserved, but what we do observe is:

$$\begin{aligned} &y = 0 \text{ if } y^* \leq 0, \\ &y = 1 \text{ if } 0 < y^* \leq \mu_1, \\ &y = 2 \text{ if } \mu_1 < y^* \leq \mu_2, \\ &y = 3 \text{ if } \mu_3 \leq y^*. \end{aligned} \tag{4}$$

This is a form of censoring. The $\mu's$ are unknown parameters to be estimated with β. The choice of the respondents follows a decision-making process which depends on certain measurable factors, x, and certain unobservable factors, ε. In the ordered probit model, ε has a standard normal distribution. The probability of observing outcome i corresponds to the probability that the estimated linear function, plus random error, is within the range of the cut-points estimated in the outcome:

$$\begin{aligned} &\Pr(y=0) = \Phi(\kappa_0 - \beta' x + \mu_0) \\ &\Pr(y=1) = \Phi(\kappa_1 - \beta' x + \mu_1) - \Phi(\kappa_0 - \beta' x + \mu_0) \\ &\Pr(y=2) = \Phi(\kappa_2 - \beta' x + \mu_2) - \Phi(\kappa_1 - \beta' x + \mu_1) \\ &\Pr(y=3) = 1 - \Phi(\kappa_3 - \beta' x + \mu_3) \end{aligned} \tag{5}$$

μ_j is assumed to be normally distributed in the ordered probit. In either case, one estimates the coefficients $\beta_1, \beta_2, ..., \beta_k$ together with the cut-points $\kappa_0, \kappa_1, \kappa_2, \kappa_3$. κ_0 is taken as $-\infty$ and κ_3 is taken as $+\infty$. All of this is a direct generalization of the ordinary two-outcome probit model.

2.7 Estimation Results and Interpretation

2.7.1. Regression Estimates for the Uptake of Savings Products, Loans or Insurance

The outcome of the separate probit regressions on the determining factors of the uptake of savings products, loans and insurance is presented in Table 2.8[49].

In contrast to earlier findings in the literature from Giné et al. (2008) and (**Essay 1**, Section 1.7) we find that households may not consider financial services as an additional risk due to mistrust of the providing institution or misunmisunderstanding of the products offered, so that there may be a higher trust in MFIs in Sri Lanka than in the Ghanaian case. The higher trustworthiness of these institutions may be traced back to the more developed microfinance market and the longer existence of MFIs in Sri Lanka, which leads not only to more sustainable institutions, but also to close relationships between the institutions and the clients. In particular, households who perceived themselves as more exposed to risk, are significantly more likely to use savings products, loans or insurance, whereas the marginal effect (ME) is highest for the participation in loans, followed by savings, and insurance schemes. Poor households have a lower ability to bear a given amount of risk than their better off counterparts, so a severe shock can be ruinous for them (Ray 1999). In respect to the importance of risk coping strategies, the poor might have a higher incentive to secure against the consequences of such hazards, and so a higher probability to uptake a financial service. However, a household's self perception of risk exposure can only give an indication that its higher exposure to risk may lead to higher awareness of, and aversion towards, risks[50].

In respect to the exposure of risks experienced in the preceding five years, it depends highly on the type of past risk, whether a household is more or less likely to participate in savings, loans, or insurance schemes. Nevertheless, the risk experience in the past is associated with the uptake for savings, loans or insurance. In case of a serious drought, households are significantly less likely to

49 The coefficients are normalized to reflect the marginal effect of a one-unit change in the explanatory variable on the probability of financial service uptake. Because of the underlying cross-sectional survey data, we treat cautiously any causality of the estimation outcomes due to the inability to control for heterogeneity or potential reverse causal relationships. Further, it is important to note that our findings include potential endogeneity problems, as omitted explanatory or third factor variables also influence the outcomes and explanations shown here, so we limit our interpretations to associations.

50 Our finding is limited in explanatory power due to the subjective (perception) measurement of the type and degree of risk aversion.

use any savings products, whereas after an animal threat households are significantly more likely to use a savings product than households without such experience. The experience of a crop failure in the previous five years leads to a significantly higher likelihood of the household using credit, but a lower likelihood of requesting insurance. In line with the findings of **Essay 1** (Section 1.7) for rural Ghana, we find that households are significantly more likely to use savings products after the experience of the death of a household member, but less likely to use loans.

Table 2.8: Outcome of Separate Probit Models for the Use of Financial Services

Variable	**Use of Savings**	**Use of Loans**	**Use of Insurance**
	MEs	MEs	MEs
Household's self-perception of risk	0.323***	0.614***	0.003***
Drought	-0.773***	0.107	-0.001
Animal threat	0.518***	0.151	-0.001
Crop failure	0.190	0.722***	-0.003**
Death experience	0.409***	-0.360***	0.217
Illness experience	0.451***	-0.232	0.0001
Input	-0.946***	-0.404***	-0.003*
No ability to sell agricultural products	0.414***	0.702***	0.019
Other risk experience	0.104	0.763***	-0.004***
Female head	0.278	0.881***	0.009
Household size	-0.106	0.147***	0.004***
Age	0.131	0.214***	-0.002***
Age squared	-0.002*	-0.002***	0.00002**
No or only primary educ.	-0.821***	-0.492***	0.123
Secondary education	-0.725***	-0.239*	0.009*
Head is self-employed	0.392	-0.970***	0.002
Head is unemployed	0.627***	-0.649***	0.0003
Distance to road	-0.0004	0.0008***	0.000002
Remittance	-0.639***	0.569**	0.048
Land ownership	0.947***	0.392***	0.003
Asset index	0.221	0.309***	0.012***
Observations	330	330	330

Source: Authors' calculation.

Note: Probit models. Coefficients are normalized to display marginal effects (MEs). The asterisks indicate level of significance (Robust z-statistics): ***significant at 1 percent, ** significant at 5 percent, * significant at 10 percent.

In the case of a severe illness, we find, in contradiction to **Essay 1** (Section 1.7), that households are more likely to save and less likely to take up credit; indeed, the latter estimate is not statistically significant. After the experience of a dramatic increase in input prices, households have a statistically significant lower likelihood of using savings products, loans, or insurance, but after the occurrence of the inability to sell agricultural products, households are more likely to take up savings or loans. The idiosyncratic shocks which are accumulated in the last risk exposure dummy significantly increase the likelihood of the household's requesting loans, but decrease the likelihood of purchasing insurance. Households uses loans as an ex post risk management strategy after the experience of shocks such as crop failure, inability to sell agricultural products and other idiosyncratic hazards. All of these risks are either agriculture related or idiosyncratic risks, which may be sufficiently covered, for both the household and the providing institution, by respective credit options. However, it appears that family related shocks such as death or illness of a household member decrease the likelihood of the household using loans, as credit may lose its effectiveness as an ex post coping mechanism if the consequences of the shock are permanent. The same finding occurs for a dramatic increase in input prices.

We find that savings may function as an ex ante risk coping strategy in the case of family related shocks, such as death or illness of a household member, an animal threat or inability to sell agricultural products. The likelihood of using insurance decreases after the experience of a crop failure or an increase in input prices, but there is no evidence that households are more likely to request insurance after any such incidence. It is important to note that savings and insurance are unable to cover the costs of a shock if they are purchased after its occurrence. Furthermore, our findings might indicate that high risk households are more likely to participate in multiple financial services in advance, as they are more likely to suffer from negative shocks. This may cause adverse selection problems in the insurance market. Nevertheless, it is a plausible hypothesis that a household's financial behaviour is associated with the risk exposure of the household in the past and in the present.

We include several control variables for more aspects of the household's decision to take up savings, credit or insurance, but limit the discussion to those which appear to be statistically significant. In contrast to earlier contributions in the literature, we find that female-headed households are more likely to use loans than their male counterparts. A possible explanation might be that several MFIs, e.g. the WDF, are explicitly targeting women within their microcredit schemes in Sri Lanka. We expected household size to be a significant determinant for a household's uptake of savings products, credit or insurance. In fact, it is evident that, with increasing household size, a household requests more loans or insurance policies. This suggests that household heads in larger households feel more responsible and have higher incentives to protect the other members of the household than heads in smaller households.

Age is intimately related to credit and insurance uptake in significant ways. In line with earlier findings in the literature, we find a life-cycle effect for the use of loans, due to the longer lifetime experience with financial services and more developed economic activities, but not for insurance participation. The turning point for credit uptake is 53 years of age, indicating that the need and respectively the access to credit decreases in old age. The turning point for insurance uptake is 58 years of age. With increasing age, household heads obviously request less insurance, but from the turning point onwards they request more. This indicates that younger household heads request more insurance since they have more experience with financial matters due to their more developed economic activities, or they have more knowledge of financial markets and insurance due to higher educational attainment than older household heads. Thus, it seems that younger household heads are more financially capable than older ones.

Echoing previous contributions in the literature, household heads with no formal primary or secondary education are significantly less likely to use savings products or loans than their better educated counterparts. We find a marginally positive relation between insurance uptake and the secondary education level of the household head[51]. Our results suggest that lower levels of educational attainment reduce the probability of using financial services. Households with a lower educational level are obviously less financially capable, due to their lower cognitive ability, to understand financial products and markets, and so have less willingness to experiment with them.

As we expected, we find that households with a head who is either self-employed or unemployed are significantly less likely to use credit; consequently, household heads with lower income earning abilities due to self-employment or unemployment lack access to loans, compared to employed heads or heads being employers with respective higher income earning abilities.

We find that remittances significantly increase the likelihood of savings and decrease that of loan uptake. This suggests that remittances represent an additional income source and form of collateral, thereby facilitating a household's access to loans. In contrast to an earlier finding from **Essay 1** (Section 1.7) for rural Ghana, remittances may function as a substitute for savings products here.

51 It might be better to use number of years of schooling to control for the educational level instead of the three educational dummies, but the underlying survey did not collect such information.

Being an indication of socioeconomic status, we assume that households which own land or have a higher asset endowment are more likely to use savings products, loans or insurance[52]. Our findings confirm that better off households are more likely to use savings, loans or insurance. This implies that the poorest households are excluded from the use of financial services, or that they have no or only limited access to them. There might also exist price or non-price obstacles to finance for the poor in Sri Lanka.

2.7.2. Regression Estimates for the Use of Zero, One, Two or Three Financial Services

In Table 2.9 and Table 2.10 we estimate an ordered probit model on the uptake of zero, one, two or three financial services to derive which role financial services can play in terms of risk mitigation and financial capability in Sri Lanka[53]. In Table 2.10, we replace the explanatory variable "asset index" with five asset quintiles indicating a household's relative wealth status rank in terms of asset endowment to investigate in more detail whether the poor have access to financial services or not and whether financial service providers successfully target the poor. In comparison, we present regression estimates of probit models for the use of specific combinations of financial services (Table 2.11)[54].

In line with the previous outcome of the probit regressions (Table 2.8), we find that households who perceived themselves as being more exposed to risk, are more likely to request one, two or three financial services, although the latter is statistically insignificant. Those more exposed households are significantly less likely to use no financial service.

---

52 A household's income is not included as an explanatory variable, but we assume that better off households, due to a higher asset endowment and land ownership, have a higher ability to generate income.

53 The coefficients are normalized to reflect the marginal effect of a one-unit change in the explanatory variable on the probability of financial service uptake. We calculated the marginal effects for the ordered probit estimation using the *margeff* command in Stata (Bartus 2005). Average marginal effects and standard errors for marginal effects are calculated using the delta method.

54 These findings give an indication of what the determinants of the use of specific combinations of financial services are, and can be used to enhance the discussion of the ordered probit results. The combinations are savings and credit, savings and insurance, credit and insurance, and all three financial services.

Table 2.9: Ordered Probit Model on the Uptake of Financial Services (I)

Variable	**No Service** MEs	**One** MEs	**Two** MEs	**Three** MEs
Household's self-perception of risk	-0.0122*	0.0098*	0.0022*	0.0001
Drought	0.0132	-0.0106	-0.0025	-0.0001
Animal threat	-0.005	0.0048	0.0010	0.00005
Crop failure	0.0151	-0.0121	-0.0028	-0.0002
Death experience	-0.0361***	0.0301***	0.0058***	0.0003**
Illness experience	-0.0387***	0.0321***	0.0063***	0.0003**
Input	-0.0183	0.0151	0.0031	0.0002
No ability to sell agricultural products	-0.0408***	0.0342***	0.0063***	0.0003**
Other risk experience	-0.0069	0.0057	0.0012	0.00006
Female head	-0.0047	0.0038	0.0008	0.00004
Household size	-0.0044	0.0036	0.0008	0.0004*
Age	-0.0056	0.0045	0.0010	0.00005
Age squared	0.00006	-0.00005	-0.00001	-0.0000005
No or only primary education	0.0049	-0.0040	-0.0009	-0.00005
Secondary education	0.0008	-0.0007	-0.0002	-0.0000008
Head is self-employed	0.0159	-0.0129	-0.0028	-0.0001
Head is unemployed	0.0162	-0.0130	-0.0030	-0.0002
Distance to road	0.0000009	-0.0000008	-0.0000002	-0.000000009
Remittance	-0.0205	0.0168	0.0035	0.0002
Land ownership	-0.0598***	0.0483***	0.0109***	0.0006***
Asset index	-0.0318***	0.0258***	0.0058***	0.0003**
Observations	330			

Source: Authors' calculation.

Note: Ordered probit model. Coefficients are normalized to display marginal effects (MEs). The asterisks indicate level of significance (Robust z-statistics): ***significant at 1 percent, ** significant at 5 percent, * significant at 10 percent.

Table 2.11 also shows a positive association with a household's participation in savings and loans, savings and insurance, loans and insurance, and all three of these. This indicates that the uptake of financial services increases with a household's subjective perception of risk, so that households may not link financial service uptake with an additional risk, but consider such services as adequate coping measures. It seems that household heads use different combinations of financial products related to their financial capability level as a response to the incidence of a peril. The poor are obviously more exposed to risks, so it appears that they have a higher incentive to secure against future shocks and thus, have a higher probability to uptake a financial service, even if this uptake is constrained by a limited access to financial services.

In line with the findings from the previous probit regression models, the experience of specific hazards in the past is associated with the probability of the uptake for one, two or three financial services (Table 2.9). The same is true for the estimates for the combinations of financial services in the separate probit model (Table 2.11). We confirm that, after a death experience, households are significantly more likely to request one, two or three financial services. The same result appears in the case of severe illness of a household member. The inability to sell agricultural products in the previous five years is negatively associated with the use of no service, but positively with the household's request for one, two or three financial services. This underlines the fact that households might use one or a more diversified set of financial services as risk coping mechanisms after the experience of certain shocks.

The death and severe illness of a household member, as both are family related and idiosyncratic hazards, may be covered by specific financial services, such as savings and insurance, if these services were contracted before the incidence of the risk. Furthermore, credit may be unable to cover the long-term costs of permanent shocks, so it is possible that credit would cover, for instance, funeral expenses, but not the loss of monthly income streams in the case of the breadwinner's death. The inability to sell agricultural goods can be rather an idiosyncratic or aggregate hazard depending on the reason for the inability to sell. Interestingly, a household's accessibility to financial services and its probability of using all three financial services decreases after the experience of a crop failure or other shock (Table 2.9). In sum, it is important to note that high-risk households may be more likely to participate in advance in multiple financial services, which may lead to adverse selection problems in the insurance market. Nevertheless, there is significant evidence of the association between financial behaviour and the past risk exposure of the households.

In the following, we emphasize the statistically significant control variables covering more characteristics of the household's decision to use financial services. We find that larger households are more likely to access the financial market and use financial services, as they are more concerned with protecting their members from possible harm.

Table 2.10: Ordered Probit Model on the Uptake of Financial Services (II)

Variable	**No Service** MEs	**One** MEs	**Two** MEs	**Three** MEs
Household's self-perception of risk	-0.0288**	0.0196**	0.0084**	0.0009
Drought	0.0434	-0.0286	-0.0132	-0.0016
Animal threat	-0.0052	0.0035	0.0015	0.0002
Crop failure	0.0249	-0.0165	-0.0075	-0.0009
Death experience	-0.0823**	0.0591**	0.0213***	0.0019**
Illness experience	-0.0927***	0.0663***	0.0242***	0.0023***
Input	-0.0441	0.0307	0.0121	0.0012
No ability to sell agricultural products	-0.1104***	0.0810***	0.0271***	0.0023***
Other risk experience	-0.0093	0.0063	0.0027	0.0003
Female head	-0.0000003	-0.0000002	0.00000008	0.00000008
Household size	-0.0107	0.0073	0.0311	0.0003
Age	-0.0109	0.0074	0.0032	0.0003
Age squared	0.0001	-0.00008	-0.00004	-0.0000004
No or only primary education	0.0156	-0.0105	-0.0046	-0.0005
Secondary education	0.0059	-0.0041	-0.0017	-0.0002
Head is self-employed	0.0307	-0.0209	-0.0088	-0.0009
Head is unemployed	0.0317	-0.0212	-0.0094	-0.0011
Distance to road	0.00002	-0.00001	-0.0000005	-0.00000006
Remittance	-0.0509	0.0357	0.0138	0.0013
Land ownership	-0.1248***	0.0823***	0.0379***	0.0041***
Quintile 1	0.1382***	-0.1155***	-0.0597**	-0.0081
Quintile 2	0.1357**	-0.0875***	-0.0429*	-0.0054
Quintile 3	0.0122	-0.0082	-0.0036	-0.0004
Quintile 4	-0.0129	0.0088	0.0037	0.0004
Observations	330			

Source: Authors' calculation.

Note: Ordered probit model. Coefficients are normalized to display marginal effects (MEs). The asterisks indicate level of significance (Robust z-statistics): ***significant at 1 percent, ** significant at 5 percent, * significant at 10 percent.

Table 2.11: Probit Models on the Uptake of Financial Services

Variable	Savings and Loan	Savings and Insurance	Loan and Insurance	Savings, Insurance and Loan
	MEs	MEs	MEs	MEs
Household's self-perception of risk	0.0903**	0.0012**	0.0021***	0.0008**
Drought	0.2415	-0.0007	-0.0008	-0.0003
Animal threat	-0.0008	0.0003	-0.0013	0.0005
Crop failure	0.7625***	-0.0012**	-0.0021	-0.0010**
Death experience	-0.0392***	0.0475	0.0623	0.0101
Illness experience	0.0028	0.0016	0.0028	0.0028
Input	-0.1848***	-0.0009	-0.0026*	-0.0003
No ability to sell agricultural products	0.4044	0.0206	0.0313	0.0118
Other risk experience	0.3482*	-0.0015**	-0.0036***	-0.011**
Female head	0.1385	0.0009	0.0040	0.0013
Household size	0.0262*	0.0011*	0.0035***	0.0008*
Age	0.033**	-0.0009**	-0.0014*	-0.0005*
Age squared	-0.0003**	0.0000008**	0.00001	0.0000005*
No or only primary educa-	-0.0639***	0.0270	0.0626	0.0178
Secondary education	-0.1077**	0.0031	0.0049	0.0024
Head is self-employed	-0.2895**	-0.0003	0.0019	0.0002
Head is unemployed	-0.0760**	-0.0014	0.0008	-0.0009
Distance to road	0.0001**	0.00000006	0.00000005	0.00000004
Remittance	0.1025	0.0023	0.0161	0.0043
Land ownership	0.1353***	0.0014	0.0028*	0.0013*
Asset index	0.0621***	0.0045***	0.0087***	0.0033***
Observations	133	152	168	108

Source: Authors' calculation.

Note: Probit models. Coefficients are normalized to display marginal effects (MEs). The asterisks indicate level of significance (Robust z-statistics): ***significant at 1 percent, ** significant at 5 percent, * significant at 10 percent.

This is shown by a positive association between household size and the outcome for three financial services, as well as for the combined use of savings products and loans, savings products and insurance, loans and insurance (Table 2.11). It seems that larger households have more economically active adult household members, indicating the higher financial resources of those households in Sri Lanka.

In line with the previous finding of a life-cycle effect for credit uptake, there is a life-cycle effect for one, two, and three financial services uptake, but none of the estimates is statistically significant (Table 2.9). However, age is a positive and significant factor regarding the uptake of savings products and credit, but negative regarding the uptake of savings products and insurance, insurance and credit, and all three financial services (Table 2.11). This indicates that household heads with increasing age are less financially capable of using a more diversified set of financial services than their younger counterparts or are restricted from access to them. Further, there appears to be a life-cycle effect for the usage of savings products and credit.

Household heads with no formal, primary or secondary education are significantly more likely to use no financial services or are excluded from the uptake of financial services than their better educated counterparts, although the marginal effects are not statistically significant. Indeed, we find that household heads with no formal, primary or secondary education are significantly less likely to request a combination of savings products and credit (Table 2.11). Households heads' lower educational attainment limits their ability to understand and apply for such services (i.e. this represents their lower financial capability), their perception of possible risk coping strategies, and also increases mistrust according to the level of participation in microfinance services and institutions. Further, they might be excluded due to lower income earning abilities and an accompanying lower socioeconomic status.

As we expected, a household's socioeconomic status is closely related to its participation in financial services in Sri Lanka. We find that households in possession of land are significantly less likely to use no financial services and more likely to request one, two, or three financial services. The same is true for households with a higher asset endowment (Table 2.9). In Table 2.11, there is evidence that the poor have a lower accessibility to specific combinations of the three financial services. In line with the literature, this indicates that microfinancial services are so far not able to target the poorest households adequately or rather the poorest have no or only limited access to such financial services in Sri Lanka (Hulme and Mosley 1997, Navajas et al. 2002, Datta 2004).

Regarding the five asset quintiles (Table 2.10), households in the two poorest quintiles (Quintile 1 and 2) are significantly more likely to be excluded from the use of financial services, but less likely to use one, two or three financial services compared to the households in the wealthiest (fifth) quintile. Having said that, we conclude that access to finance is restricted for the poorest in Sri Lanka. Exclusion can be voluntarily or involuntarily. However, it is rather unlikely that the poor choose not to use financial services. Yet, it appears that they might not use financial services due to lower financial capability levels or to religious or cultural reasons. It seems that the poor are missing a basic level of financial capability for participation in financial schemes or do not know someone who understands the services which are available for them, and who is able to fill in the required application forms (World Bank 2008). Importantly, they might also be excluded from the use of financial services because of specific requirements of the providers, like price or non-price barriers, the underlying contractual or informational frameworks, discrimination against certain population groups or the fact that they are considered to be unbankable because of low or irregular income or because they are considered to represent too high a risk (World Bank 2008).

2.8 Conclusion

Microfinancial services are promising measures for providing low-income households with different options to cope with risks of the occurrence of severe hazards. Therefore, we argue that, particularly the more diversified participation, i.e. the use of different types of financial services, holds the promise of adequately addressing the financial needs of households relative to the consequences of certain risks. It is the objective of this paper to contribute to the literature on the determinants of households' participation in microfinancial services by analyzing a household's decision to use zero, one, two or all three financial services. Using an ordered probit model, the estimation procedure allows us to test, whether a past shock experience of a household is associated with the use of financial services, and whether households identify financial services as possible risk coping mechanisms in Sri Lanka.

We conclude that the probability to uptake financial services, i.e. the request for one, two or three financial services, increases with the household's increased self-perception of risk. In contrast to the Ghanaian case in **Essay 1**, it seems that households may not link financial service uptake with an additional risk, but may instead consider them as diversified coping measures. This may indicate that households assess the MFIs in Sri Lanka as being more reliable than in Ghana. It is possible that combinations of different financial products play a key role, as a more diversified portfolio of coping mechanisms leads to a better assurance against future harm. Even though the poor are more in need of insurance against possible risk consequences, the access to financial services is still limited for them. Policy makers have to set the right legal frameworks and incentives to overcome these constraints and reach a higher geographical coverage and diversity in the financial and microfinance market.

Interestingly, the correlates of the eight dummy variables representing the households' risk exposure in the past five years give a manifold picture. It appears that the probability of the uptake for one, two or three financial services is associated with the experience of specific hazards in the past. The experience of a death, a severe illness of a household member or an inability to sell agricultural products, is positively associated with the participation in one, two or three financial services. It depends on the type of shock, i.e. permanent or transient, whether the costs of the shock can be efficiently covered by respective financial services. Therefore, financial services might be achievable and efficient risk management mechanisms implemented in Sri Lanka. Beyond our valuable insights, future research is necessary to estimate the causal impact of risk exposure on financial behaviour, taking the exact date of risk incidence and contract of financial services into account.

We elaborate some different and novel implications of particular relevance for the discussion of factors determining participation in microfinancial services. In larger households, heads are more likely to request financial services linked to higher incentives for the protection of the household. We find a life-cycle effect for the usage of credit, and for the combination of savings products and credit.

Lower educational attainment is negatively associated with the uptake of savings, credit and the combination of savings and credit, which indicates a lacking basic level of financial capability for such households. In contrast to earlier findings in the literature, remittances may function as a substitute for savings products. Finally, microfinancial services are either so far not able to reach the poorest, or the access to finance is still limited for them in Sri Lanka. It is rather unlikely that the poor choose voluntarily not to use financial services due to their high risk exposure. On the one hand, there are some households among the poor who refuse the use of financial services out of respect to religious or cultural reasons. However, on the other side the majority of the poor is still excluded from financial markets because of supply-side constraints and their poor understanding of financial services.

Having said that, it would be necessary to broaden the access to finance for the poor and especially to raise the level of knowledge among low-educated, illiterate and certain religious groups to increase the awareness of the benefits of financial services as efficient risk coping strategies. In addition, we hope to see more research on the financial capability level, using a more holistic concept of financial capability for further analyses of microfinancial services in developing countries (Kempson 2009). Moreover, it would be desirable that policy makers promote households' financial capability by increasing the public awareness of these issues and by implementing financial educational campaigns. Indeed, simple and easily understandable products and more detailed, educational information about product details, and the duties and rights of the clients are urgently demanded from the MFIs in order to empower the poor to use microfinancial services.

Essay 3

3. Participation in micro life insurance: the role of bequest motives in Sri Lanka

Abstract:

This paper examines bequest motives by evaluating participation patterns in micro life insurance against the predictions of a theoretical framework on the demand for life insurance and in relation to additional supply side factors. On household survey data from Sri Lanka, it presents evidence on the determinants of micro life insurance participation of low-income households using probit and tobit models. The results provide evidence that micro life insurance is positively correlated with measures of bequest motives, like number of children or dependents. In addition, better off households are less excluded from life insurance markets than their poorer counterparts; thus, access to micro life insurance is still limited for the poor. It appears that participation patterns go beyond the propositions of the theoretical framework; for instance, the outcome underlines the fact that the religious inclination of the underlying sample is associated with participation in micro life insurance schemes.

3.1 Introduction

In developing countries microinsurance has become a rising star, as it is increasingly recognized as an integral element of poverty reduction strategies. Due to limited resources, the adverse effects of unexpected events have a significant effect on the income of the poor, so it is hard for them to recover from these. A high potential for microinsurance is identified as a measure to reduce the vulnerabilities of low-income groups. However, many low-income households do not have the ability to use ex ante preventive risk management strategies or rely on informal mechanisms providing only partial insurance, so that they lack sufficient options to secure against hazards (Loewe et al. 2001, Cohen et al. 2005, McCord et al. 2006).

Shocks to a household's income, such as the death or illness of a household member, generate movements in consumption for households that are not perfectly insured against such risks, and, in the most extreme cases, may lead to famine or death. In the case of such family related shocks, microinsurance functions directly as a risk coping mechanism incorporating measures for consumption smoothing. After a sudden drop in income due to a recently experienced serious crisis, a household would be expected to be less likely to take up insurance. However, in a long-term perspective, we assume that the experience of a serious event in the near past induces the household to buy insurance to prevent any such recurrence. At the same time, it is clear that insurance is only one of many possible ways of reducing the impact of risk on poverty. In fact, other financial services may be beneficial as well, i.e. flexible savings products or a variety of credit options.

While other types of insurance are also relevant for the low-income market, we focus on the risk of death, which is frequently identified – along with illness – as the most severe hazard in demand research. A study of "The Landscape of Microinsurance in the World's 100 Poorest Countries" identifies life insurance as the most widely provided microinsurance policy in the world (Roth et al. 2007)[55]. Life insurance policies are financial products that mainly consist of two different components: income replacement in the event of premature death, and a long-term savings instrument. Therefore, life insurance encourages long-term savings and the reinvestment of substantial sums in private and public sector projects, and has taken on increasing importance as a way for households to manage income risks. Furthermore, the idea of life insurance is greatly welcomed by clients, supplanting private efforts to insure against loss by joining informal burial societies that pool resources and pay out to participants in the event of a loss.

Nevertheless, the debate on the demand for formal insurance in developing countries is rarely spread in the literature except for various studies on informal insurance (Townsend 1995, Morduch 1995, 1999, Dercon 2002, Churchill 2006). However, a few studies exist which use quantitative data from household surveys to identify and analyse the determinants of insurance participation (Asfaw 2003, Jütting 2003, Bhat and Jain 2006, Giné et al. 2008, Cole et al. 2009, Giné and Yang 2009, Ito and Kono 2010). It is the aim of this paper to add to these contributions on the cross-sectional determinants of microinsurance participation of low-income households, using comprehensive household survey data from Sri Lanka. Our approach is different from these discussions in the following way.

First, we assess – similarly to **Essay 1** for Ghana – the participation in micro life insurance schemes in Sri Lanka, as there are so far mainly contributions on weather, crop or health insurance. Second, the paper is the first to evaluate micro life insurance participation patterns against a benchmark theoretical

55 Life insurance is the easiest microinsurance to provide due to certain characteristics, e.g. relatively easy to price, but health insurance is demanded the most. We are grateful to an anonymous referee for pointing this out. Even though life insurance has been most successful to date, in particular credit life insurance, health insurance plans are being tried, as well as property and crop insurance in Sri Lanka.

model, developed by Lewis (1989), on the demand for life insurance. By doing so, we aim to analyse whether micro life insurance participation is motivated – besides other determinants – by the desire to leave bequests. The benchmark model suggests that life insurance participation increases with the probability of a wage earner's death, the present value of the beneficiaries' consumption and the degree of risk aversion[56]. If the household values bequest behaviour, we argue that the present value of the beneficiaries' consumption increases with the number of dependents, i.e. micro life insurance participation increases with the number of dependents. Modelling pure term life insurances and combinations of term life insurance and savings plans, we derive bequests using a "joy-of-giving" motive. We argue that bequests can be either intended (desired) (Hurd 1987), altruistic (Tomes 1982), strategic due to self-interested exchange with one's heirs (Bernheim et al. 1985) or unintended (accidental) (Hurd 1994).

Third, we estimate the determinants for micro life insurance participation by using the actual use of micro life insurance and respective premium amounts as dependent variables in probit and tobit models. The actual use of insurance, i.e. the actual provision, is determined by the supply and demand of insurance (World Bank 2008)[57], so that we control for the access to life insurance in Sri Lanka by identifying the socioeconomic characteristics of the life insurance user and non-user. Premium expenditure has typically been used as the measure of insurance consumption and coverage in previous research in developed country contexts (Burnett and Palmer 1984, Truett and Truett 1990, Browne and Kim 1993). Premium data do not allow us to observe the actual amount of insurance coverage purchased, as the premium amount is a combined measure of price and level of coverage. Nevertheless, it gives us an indication of insurance coverage, so that the combined usage enables us to control for a more holistic picture of insurance participation, including both the insurance ownership and coverage (Beck and Webb 2002).

---

56 Furthermore, the theoretical framework suggests that life insurance participation and premiums increase with the household's income and education level, whereas they decrease with the policy loading factor and the household's wealth.

57 Users of insurance can be distinguished from non-users. Among the non-users are those who voluntarily exclude themselves from the use of insurance, such as households which do not use insurance due to cultural or religious reasons, and households who do not need or want to use insurance. The other group are the involuntarily excluded households who demand insurance, but do not have access to it because of insufficient income or high risk, discrimination due to social, religious, or ethnic grounds, restrictive contractual and informational frameworks, too high prices or inappropriate product features offered by the providers (World Bank 2008).

Our main findings are as follows. Micro life insurance is strongly related to indicators of intentional bequest motives. The results provide evidence that low-income households purchase micro life insurances to be secure in the event of the premature death of the main breadwinner. Beyond that, there are a pair of results that closely support standard findings of insurance participation. Micro life insurance is not yet able to reach the poorest households in Sri Lanka. Interestingly, religious inclination is associated with the participation in micro life insurance schemes.

The outline of the paper is as follows: Section 3.2 describes the microinsurance market, specific life insurance contract features and institutional details in Sri Lanka. Section 3.3 discusses theoretical determinants of life insurance participation, and sets out hypotheses to be tested. Section 3.4 outlines our survey and the methods used in the estimation. The descriptive statistics and the results of the estimations are discussed in Section 3.5. Section 3.6 concludes.

3.2 The Microinsurance Sector and the Role of Life insurance in Sri Lanka

Even though insurance markets are growing all over the world and in particular in developing countries, commercial insurance services are still negligible among low-income households. As part of this growth, the high potential of the microinsurance markets is increasingly recognized, not only as an important integral to reduce the vulnerabilities of the poor, but also as an emerging insurance market sector and a contributor to economic growth[58]. However, the global outreach of microinsurance is limited, so that more insight is needed into why the uptake of microinsurance among the poor is still low.

Similar to several South Asian and developing countries, Sri Lanka has, on the whole, an infant microinsurance market in terms of penetration[59] (1.48%[60]) and density [61] (16.3 US$), as it ranks 75th in terms of penetration and 82nd in

58 Large country samples for the 1960s to the 1980s demonstrate that financial sector development can have an economically significant impact on growth (Haiss and Sümegi 2006).

59 Insurance penetration is defined as the amount of the total insurance premiums expressed as a percentage of the national GDP and thus, measures the level of risk awareness of the population and the significance of insurance in the economy.

60 During the last three years, the average penetration of life insurance has ranged between 1.4 to 1.6 percent in Sri Lanka (ADB 2006).

61 Insurance density indicates how much each inhabitant of a country spends each year on insurance services and so is a measure of the maturity of the industry in the economy.

terms of density (Rajivan 2007). It is plausible that the low penetration and density, indicating limited access to and provision of insurance, might be one explanation for the as yet low outreach of insurance in Sri Lanka. Nevertheless, Roth et al. (2007) suggest that there will be a significant increase of microinsurance provision in the next few years due to three major reasons: the large interest of insurers in the low-income market, the significant demand for risk management strategies in low-income households, and strong efforts by potential intermediaries to offer microinsurance.

In Sri Lanka the origin of microinsurance schemes was in funeral aid society concepts, which provided assistance to the member and family in the case of death of a family member. In 1991, the All Lanka Mutual Assurance Organization[62] (ALMAO), one of the apex microinsurance schemes, was started by seven cooperating Funeral Aid Societies (FASs). Although 14 private insurance companies and 45 insurance brokers are registered and regulated under the Insurance Board of Sri Lanka (IBSL), unregulated organizations, like mutuals, and NGOs such as YASIRU and SEEDS, dominate the microinsurance market by offering the majority of products, mainly micro life insurance, particularly in rural areas (Enarsson and Wirén 2006, Roth et al. 2007).

Micro life insurance is the most widely provided microinsurance policy in the world; however, only 67.2 million people are so far covered in Asia (Roth et al. 2007). A number of characteristics of the life insurance business have been identified as the foremost reasons for this fact: the most demanded forms of cover relate to the importance of family related serious events, are easy to price, resistant to problems of fraud and moral hazard, and are independent of other forms of infrastructure like health facilities in the case of health insurance.

Generally speaking, life insurance as well as micro life insurance can offer two services: income replacement for premature death and a long-term savings instrument (Black and Skipper 2000, Beck and Webb 2002). Policies offering mortality coverage only are generally referred to as term life insurance[63]. Those providing a combination of mortality coverage with a savings component – called the cash value – within the same contract are known as permanent, endowment, universal or whole life insurance[64]. Policies in the second category accumulate funds – similar to a savings account with a bank – that are available

62 ALMAO is the main shareholder of SANASA.

63 Term life insurance provides temporary protection; if the policy is not renewed, the protection expires at the end of the period. Term life insurance has no cash-value or savings element.

64 In general insurance markets, especially in developed countries, there exist a multitude of variations of cash value policies.

to the policy owner. Additionally, these forms of insurance earn interest, which is returned to the consumer through policy dividends, cash on termination of the policy, or endowment sums on maturation of the policy (Black and Skipper 2000).

Even though micro life insurances have the highest outreach of the micro-insurance provision in Sri Lanka, life insurance faces a dilemma, which might be another reason for the generally low uptake of microinsurance. It appears that there is public apathy to contract life insurance, because high inflation rates have reduced the maturity value of term life insurance policies in the past. Nevertheless, there exist several microinsurance products offering death benefits, which can be viewed as a form of term life insurance, and which provide a wide variety of other schemes like accident, hospitalization, health and other benefits[65]. In the household data set used here, the predominant micro life insurance product is a term life insurance providing only mortality coverage, mainly for the policy owner. We suggest that the remaining micro life insurances can be understood as cash value policies incorporating not only substantial amounts of mortality coverage, but variable savings components as well.

However, major differences are observed in terms of premium, benefits value, duration of membership, age at entry, or in terms of the number of clients covered by a micro life insurance policy. However, except for three types of life microinsurance policies – *Sithumina, Divithura and Pilsarana,* offered by the SANASA – all other policies cover the family members as well. The WDBF and the WDF for instance, treat the whole family as the policy holder, so that the premiums vary depending on the benefits included, but not on the number of family members covered.

3.3 Modelling Life Insurance Uptake – A Conceptual Review

3.3.1. Theoretical Framework of the Demand for Life Insurance

Nearly all theoretical work on the demand for life insurance takes Yaari (1965) as a starting point, followed by the work of Hakansson (1969). In the context of

65 For instance, the YASIRU offers products with coverage for death, accident and health. The Women's Development Federation in Hambantota provides special products in addition to death, hospitalization and health products, such as marriage and childbirth. ALMAO covers death, disability, hospitalization and life savings.

a life-cycle model with uncertain lifetime, Yaari (1965) and Hakansson (1969) presented the first theoretical framework to explain the demand for life insurance. Both assume that an individual can enhance his lifetime utility by purchasing a life insurance policy and leave, as a portion of his income, a bequest sum for dependents. By examining bequest motives in considerable detail, Yaari (1965) and Hakansson (1969) find that the demand for life insurance is related to the person's desire to leave funds to dependents and/or provide income for retirement. In detail, Yaari's framework suggests that a consumer purchases life insurance to increase his expected lifetime utility, as follows:

$$E[U(T)] = \int^{T} \alpha(t) g[c(t)]dt + \beta(T)\varphi[S(T)] \qquad (1)$$

where in (1) T is the consumer's lifetime, i.e. assumed as a random variable, $\varphi[S(T)]$ is the instantaneous utility of bequests, $g[c(t)]$ is the instantaneous utility from consumption in present value, and $\alpha(.)$ and $\beta(.)$ are the discount factors. Casually observed, $\beta(.)$ rises when consumers get married or have offspring, as these events account for much of the change in life insurance ownership (Yaari 1965). Concerning the relationship in (1), fluctuations in the demand for life insurance depend mainly on exogenous shifts in the consumer's utility function. Within the models of Yaari (1965) and Hankansson (1969), the consumer maximizes lifetime utility subject to a vector of interest rates and a vector of prices including insurance premium rates, so that the demand for life insurance is a function of wealth, expected income over an individual's lifetime, the level of interest rates, and the cost of life insurance policies[66].

Based on these models, Lewis (1989) was the first who explicitly included the preferences of the dependents and beneficiaries in a model, in order to extend the theoretical framework beyond previous work[67]. This benchmark model guides our analysis. If applicable, we will modify its predictions and add some predictions, including more demand- and supply-side factors, and will compare our example taken from a developing country perspective with it.

As an extension of Yaari (1965) and Hakansson (1969), the benchmark model suggests the demand for life insurance not only as a maximization of the consumer lifetime utility, but also as a maximization problem of the beneficiaries, spouse and offspring of the life insurance policy holder. Consistent with the life insurance literature, it appears that life insurance should be purchased to satisfy the needs of survivors. The above mentioned exogenous shifts of the consumer's utility function are now assumed to be at least partly endogenous by

66 That are administrative costs, and the assumed subjective discount rate for current over future consumption.

67 Fischer (1973) also constructed a standard model of participation in life insurance markets including bequest motives, a model which is not described in detail here.

incorporating the preferences of the beneficiaries (Lewis 1989). Life insurance premiums can be also regarded as payments made by parents on behalf on their offspring, and, in that sense, are equivalent to expenditures on children's clothing or other commodities provided by the parents to the offspring.

Lewis (1989) derives utility maximization by spouse and offspring separately by assuming no inheritance from the policy holder, and by assuming an isoelastic utility function. Total life insurances taken up on the husband's life is simply the sum of the purchases by the wife and each offspring. It is assumed that each household member has the same degree of relative risk aversion and it is noted that the non-negativity constraint on life insurance holdings is binding on all or none of the household members. Following Lewis (1989), life insurance demand can be written as follows:

$$(1-lp)F = \max\{[\frac{1-lp}{l(1-p)}]^{1/\delta}TC - W, 0\} \quad (2)$$

where in (2) l is the policy loading factor, i.e. the ratio of the costs of the insurance to its actuarial value, p is the probability of the primary wage earner's death, F the face value of all life insurance written on the primary wage earner's life, δ the measure of the beneficiaries' relative risk aversion, TC the present value of consumption of each offspring until he/she leaves the household and of the spouse over his/her predicted remaining life time, and W the household's net wealth[68]. From the interrelationship in (2), the following proposition can be derived:

Proposition 1: *Life insurance participation increases with the probability of the breadwinner's death, the present value of the beneficiaries' consumption and the degree of risk aversion, whereas it decreases with the loading factor and the household's wealth.*

The Lewis model suggests that, if the present value of consumption of the beneficiaries increases, the demand for life insurance increases as well. As the present value of consumption of the beneficiaries is positively related to the number of dependents, and as life insurance provides dependents with payments in the case of the premature death of the household head (primary income earner), we argue that life insurance participation increases with the number of dependents of a policy holder or in a household which values bequests behaviour. Therefore, it could be that a higher number of young dependents, i.e. children, increases the demand for mortality coverage and decreases the demand for savings through life insurance. As young dependents emphasize precautionary motives, they may be considered to be too young to save for retirement and

68 For the probability of the primary wage earner's death and the loading factor there is no reasonable information in the data set; hence, we concentrate on the remaining predicted determining factors of the model.

reduce demand for savings through life insurance. For instance, the ratio of dependents to the total working population is expected to influence the demand for life insurance, especially the mortality coverage (Browne and Kim 1993, Beck and Webb 2002)[69]. We furthermore assume that a higher number of old dependents decreases the demand for mortality coverage and increases the demand for savings through life insurance. It is important to note that the strength and the type of the bequest motive varies over lifetime, i.e. the bequest motive decreases and the saving motive increases with increasing age, whereas the bequest motive is at its peak at the prime age of the policy holder.

Proposition 2: *Life insurance participation increases with the number of dependents in the household, whereas a higher number of young dependents increases the demand for mortality coverage and a higher number of old dependents decreases the demand for savings through life insurance.*

Besides the presence and number of children, several contributions claim that a bequest motive may result from being married (Bernheim et al. 2003, Inkmann et al. 2009). In principle, uncertain time for life, altruism, and strategic behaviour towards heirs are the three main identified reasons for making bequests. Involuntary bequests may occur depending on uncertain lifetimes and incomplete insurance markets, so uninsured risks relating to health and longevity may give rise to precautionary motives for preserving wealth in old age (Vidal-Meliá and Lejárraga-Garcia 2005). In contrast to an egoistic[70] bequest motive, the altruistic motive is motivated by the utility of the recipient, i.e. the policy holder simply wants to leave a bequest to his family (Tomes 1982, Bernheim 1991), whereas the strategic motive is motivated by the desire to manipulate the behaviour of the recipient, i.e. to give an incentive to look after the policy holder in his old age by promising a bequest in return (Bernheim et al. 1985). Our case includes information on term life, but as well on cash value insurances, although we expect that in the latter savings motives play a larger role than precautionary motives. While term life insurance is strongly related to precautionary motives, i.e. the existence of bequest motives (Inkmann and Michaelides 2010), we focus on the precautionary motives, as term life insurances predominate in our data source.

---

69 Beck and Webb (2002) derive different further variables determining the demand for life insurance that may be related or based on the demand function described by Lewis (1989). They present variables not only on the individual (or household) level, but as well on the institutional and macroeconomic level, which we do not discuss in detail here or, if applicable, we attempt to link to the household instead country level.

70 The bequest motive can be egoistic in that it can be generated purely by a desire to have positive net worth upon death.

The benchmark model predicts that the willingness to pay for security fundamentally depends on the degree of risk aversion of the household. Arrow (1965) and Pratt (1964) find the commonly well-accepted hypothesis that the absolute risk aversion decreases with the increasing wealth of an individual. In a developed country context, there is evidence that individuals without life insurance are significantly less risk averse than their counterparts with life insurance, whereas the risk aversion increases with the income and wealth up to a mean of the respective distribution, and then decreases (Barsky et al. 1997). This indicates a life-cycle effect of the degree of an individual's risk aversion, whereas the latter decreases after a certain amount of wealth, income or age. It is plausible to suggest that better off households have a better ability and willingness to bear a given amount of risk compared to relatively poor households. As the poor are too close to subsistence in developing countries, a given loss can be ruinous for them, so that they are most risk averse (Ray 1999). Thus, we suggest a positive association between the uptake of life insurance and the degree of risk aversion in Sri Lanka.

Beyond this model's prediction is the possibility that religious inclination may affect the uptake of life insurance, as the degree of risk aversion and the attitude towards life insurance depend highly on the country's culture and the predominant religion (Browne and Kim 1993)[71]. In several Islamic countries, life insurance has been traditionally disapproved of, as it is seen as a hedge against the will of Allah (Beck and Webb 2002). In Sri Lanka, the predominant religion is Buddhist, followed by Islam, Hindu and Christians[72]. As there are no Islamic households in our data set, we neglect expectations due to Islamic inclination here. We employ a broader measure of religious inclination, which includes the other three prevalent religious beliefs. As so far there exist no contributions on the effect of religious differences on insurance participation for these groups, we do not have prior expectations about the effects the religious correlates.

---

71 Historically, religion has been a strong source of cultural opposition to life insurance, as uptake of life insurance relies on a distrust of God's protecting care (Zelizer 1979). Until the 19th century, life insurance policies and companies were condemned for religious reasons.

72 72.6 percentage of the population are Buddhist, followed by 10.8 percentage of Islam, 9.2 percentage of Hindu and 7.3 percentage of Christian (The Department of Census & Statistics Sri Lanka 2008). The majority of the Hindu population belongs to the ethnic group of Sri Lankan native Tamil, who are mainly located in the Northern and North-Eastern provinces of Sri Lanka.

Proposition 3: *Religious inclination may affect a household's willingness to participate in a life insurance scheme.*

In principle, education may have an effect of increasing the time period of dependency, which may increase the demand for mortality coverage, so that a higher level of education is assumed to be positively correlated with the use of life insurance (Beck and Webb 2002). It could be, that, on the one hand, it may raise the ability to understand the benefits of risk management and savings, but on the other hand, it may also increase the individual's risk aversion, which would be reflected by a lower δ in the Lewis model (Beck and Webb 2002). We argue that life insurance participation may increase with the level of income, due to increasing consumption and human capital, i.e. this creates a higher demand for mortality coverage in order to preserve the income and consumption of household head and dependents. This has been shown by using individual household data for both developed and developing countries by Lewis (1989), Truett and Truett (1990), Browne and Kim (1993) and Outreville (1996). However, it is plausible that there may exist an opposite effect, as poor households are more risk averse than better off ones, and thus are more in need of life insurance. We control for this possibility in our estimations.

Proposition 4: *Life insurance participation increases with the household's income and education level.*

Represented by the policy loading factor in the model, supply side factors affect the cost of life insurance products and the consumption of life insurance (Beck and Webb 2002). First, the investment function of life insurers is facilitated by an adequate protection of property rights and an effective enforcement of contracts. Second, the insurer is in need of adequate human and information resources for effective pricing measurement, for the reservation of product requirements, as well as for adequate investment opportunities in the financial market. Both directly influence the costs of life insurance products for the insurer. Third, it is obvious that many households remain uninsured against significant income risks due to various reasons; thus, adverse selection and moral hazard are largely considered as potential explanations for barriers to insurance participation (Rothschild and Stiglitz 1976, Cawley and Phillipson 1999).

Contrary to the separating equilibrium in Rothschild and Stiglitz (1976), Cawley and Philipson (1999) note that, conditional on observables, life insurance premia decrease in the quantity of insurance purchased. Models of adverse selection and moral hazard are applicable to the life insurance contracts studied here. In practice, life expectancy is public information, but the individual's health status, life expectancy and accident probability are not totally observable by the insurance provider or, if so, only with a high investment in time, costs and human resources. Thus, we argue that the insurance providing institution cannot fully determine whether an individual is at high or low risk of death, so that adverse selection may occur in the life insurance market. Ito and Kono (2010) find some evidence of the existence of adverse selection in micro health insurance provision in India, as households having a higher ratio of sick members are more likely to purchase microinsurance, which leads to practical problems in insurance participation. Theoretically, moral hazard may exist as well in the context of life insurance markets, this being the case if the household may live with less caution and risk more after contracting insurance.

3.3.2. Empirical Findings on Insurance Participation from Developing Countries

Differing from the benchmark model of life insurance, we add here empirical evidence on non-life insurance participation, namely health or rainfall insurance, in order to derive additional expectations on participation patterns from a developing country context.

As many low-income households do not have the ability to use ex ante preventive risk management strategies or lack sufficient options to secure against hazards, numerous studies point out that there exists high potential for (micro)insurance in developing countries (Loewe et al. 2001, Cohen et al. 2005, McCord et al. 2006). However, there are, to our knowledge, so far only a few studies using quantitative data from household surveys to identify and analyse determinants of the usage of formal insurance (Asfaw 2003, Jütting 2003, Bhat and Jain 2006, Giné et al. 2008, Cole et al. 2009, Giné and Yang 2009, Ito and Kono 2010). All studies emphasize the impact of various demographic household characteristics and the risk exposure of the household. Empirical evidence has shown that a household is more likely to contract insurance with its increasing income and expected loss payments (Jütting 2003, Pauly 2004, Bhat and Jain 2006, Giné et al. 2008). In contrast to developed countries, Giné et al. (2008) find that risk averse households are less likely to purchase insurance due to supply side constraints, i.e. the risk averse low-income households do not have access to insurance. Furthermore, households with a higher risk exposure or which feel more exposed to risk have a lower probability of participating in micro life insurance (**Essay 1** for Ghana, Section 1.7); nevertheless, **Essay 2** for Sri Lanka (Section 2.7.2) shows the opposite, as here the households are more likely to use a more diversified set of financial serivces. The two prior findings reflect the uncertainty about the offered product itself and especially the lack of understanding of the insurance concept and the mechanism behind insurance

(McCord 2001, Chankova et al. 2008). It is possible that it depends on the reliability of the providing institution and its educational efforts, whether households view insurance as a risky option for them.

An often identified barrier in the distribution of insurance to low-income households is their lack of understanding of insurance schemes (McCord 2001). More educated households have been found to be the ones which are more likely to take up insurance (Chankova et al. 2008, Giné et al. 2008). Overcoming this constraint requires a dual effort, targeted at low-educated and illiterate individuals, to improve communication and financial education on risk-pooling, insurance and the rights of policy holders on the one hand, while simplifying policies on the other (McCord 2001).

The exposure to shocks has an impact on the uptake of financial services, but it depends on the type of risk (**Essay 1**, Section 1.7, **Essay 2**, Section 2.7). Moreover, an important role in insurance participation is the trust of the client in the providing institution (Cole et al. 2009). For customer retention, it is important that the insurer proves trust along two dimensions: first, that the insurer is willing to make payments to clients, and second, that the insurer is able to deliver the payments (Radermacher et al. 2006). However, there is so far little systematic knowledge about instruments and mechanisms for building trust (Schneider 2005). In an environment where a product is new and not well understood, it seems plausible that households will draw inferences based on their degree of experience and familiarity with the insurance providing institution. These inferences may be closely linked to the household's ability to rely on information gleaned from social networks, such as other trusted households which purchase insurance.

As noted above, households may differ in their ability to understand an insurance product, for instance life insurance, as well as in their willingness to experiment with it[73]. Therefore, we assume that younger and more educated household heads are more likely to understand such a product more easily, and to be more likely to participate in such schemes than their older and less educated counterparts. Dror et al. (2007) find that there is a higher level of nominal willingness to pay for micro health insurance compared to the findings of previous studies, and that household income and nominal willingness to pay for insurance are positively correlated (while household's income and willingness to pay as a percentage of household income are negatively correlated). It is im-

73 The ability to understand insurance concepts is not only limited to lower educated households, even well educated individuals find it hard to understand complex products as most insurers do not try to clarify or simplify the product details and the functioning of insurance. We are grateful to an an, but tend to obfuscate, use fine print and protect themselves.

portant to note that household size is the most important determinant of willingness to pay for micro health insurance (Dror et al. 2007). In sum, we expect a positive relationship between the willingness to pay for micro life insurance in low-income households with their level of income and education, household size, understanding of the insurance concept and trust in the providing tion, but a negative one with the degree of risk aversion.

3.4 Data and Methodology

3.4.1. Data

The data for the analysis in this paper comes from a household survey conducted from May to July in 2008 in various villages covering all districts and regions in Sri Lanka[74]. In total, 330 households were interviewed, including two strata of (micro)insured and non-insured households. All households within each stratum were chosen through random sampling. Out of these households, 240 households have bought and 90 have not bought any insurance. The providers surveyed offer insurance in various stylized forms for different types of risk to which households may be exposed in the future[75]. It is important to note that – although we focus on life insurance – there are major differences between life insurance and other insurance types like health, property or crop insurance. Detailed sections on demographic and socioeconomic household characteristics, household assets, the occurrence of shocks, risk management strategies, and the evaluation of a household's subjective perception of its risk exposure and situation, were included in the survey questionnaire, which emphasized the household's integration in financial markets and its participation in loans and savings products, in particular life insurance.

Five different MFIs, namely the WDF, the WDBF, SANASA, YASIRU and SEEDS had been identified in advance as the main providers of voluntary[76] microinsurance for low-income households in Sri Lanka and these were used to select the insured households (see Table 3.1). The number of total households –

74 The survey was conceived in the context of a research project on the demand for microinsurance among low-income households in Sri Lanka.

75 In the household data set, there are eight different insurance types: (1) health insurance, (2) life insurance, (3) other life-cycle event insurance, (4) vehicle insurance, (5) old age annuities/pension, (6) credit insurance, (7) crop insurance and (8) property insurance.

76 The participating institutions provide credit life insurance as well, which is compulsory for the uptake of a loan or other financial product. Yet, these credit insurances are not considered in this study and the respective observations have been dropped from the data set.

insured and non-insured – selected from the villages which were linked to the outreach of one of the five institutions differs; in total, only 40 households – insured and non-insured – were linked to the villages and districts where the WDF operates (i.e. Hambantota), while 95 households were associated with the outreach area of SEEDS, as SEEDS operates in all districts in the country. 65 households were related to the coverage areas of the other three institutions (i.e. YASIRU, the WDBF and SANASA).

The survey sampling frame is a census of households across 30 villages covering all 14 districts in which these MFIs operate in Sri Lanka. From each district, two or three MFIs have been selected, except for the districts Vavuniya and Batticaloa, located in the Northern and Eastern provinces, where only SEEDS is present. The selected number of insured and non-insured households from each district varied from 15 to 50.

We used the client bases of the five MFIs to randomly select the households for the insured strata. The chosen number of households covered by each institution were randomly spread across the districts in which they operate. In consultation with the district branch managers and respective staff members, we selected two or three villages for each district, representing the respective MFIs in the district, so that access to a high density of insured households could be ensured. From each village, 10 to 15 insured and non-insured households were covered. As we included 30 villages in total all over Sri Lanka, we assume our results to be representative for all villages in Sri Lanka at least, in which microinsurance is accessible via the selected MFIs.

Table 3.1: Number of All Insured Clients and Insured Clients Surveyed in the Five MFIs

Number of	Total Clients	Total Insured	Insured Surveyed
WDF	44,000	11,000	29
WDBF	50,000	10,000	48
SANASA	20,184	20,184	51
YASIRU	21,000	21,000	47
SEEDS	476,443	179,516	65
Total	611,627	241,800	240

Source: Authors' calculation.

The selected villages may be seen as typical villages in rural and semi-urban areas in Sri Lanka. The livelihood activities of most of the households in these villages are agriculture activities, fishery, craft and related works, work as plant and machine operators and assemblers, and other forms of basic or low-skilled occupation, so that the nature of the livelihood activities may be seen as another reason for a household's vulnerability. Therefore, our results might be replicable in any other village in Sri Lanka, besides large cities or remote areas with limited access to microfinance, so that the generalisation might have greater applicability, even though external validity is not fully secured.

We did not select the non-insured clients directly from the client base of the MFIs. The non-insured had to be randomly picked from lists of households from existing CBOs, which are not exclusively associated with any of the five MFIs, in the villages, because of limited financial resources for the survey. For each village one CBO was picked randomly from a list of existing CBOs created with the help of the branch manager and the staff members of the MFIs in the district.

In our estimations we use "purchased life insurance" or "premium amount of purchased life insurance" as the dependent variables and estimate probit regressions[77], using sampling weights to control for varying sampling probabilities[78]. All analyses were performed in Intercooled Stata 10.0. Table C. 1 (in Appendix C) shows the definition and specific details of each variable's construction expressed as an independent variable[79]. We calculated variance inflation factors (VIFs) to test for possible collinearity among independent variables, but found no substantial concerns[80]. In the estimations, the vector of explanatory variables includes different household characteristics, including demographic and wealth variables such as bequest motives, education, economic activities of the household head, the distance to a road as an access to market indicator, information about remittances, a self perception index of risk

77 The probit regressions are estimated by using the STATA survey data command *svy*.

78 The weights of the insured strata are computed as the relation between the insured households surveyed and the total number of insured clients for each of the five MFIs (see Table 3.1). The weights of the non-insured strata cannot be calculated in an analogous manner, as SANASA and YASIRU are exclusive insurers. Therefore, due to the missing information on the total number of non-insured households, we use the listed non-insured households from the CBOs in the villages as representatives of the total non-insured households surveyed. By doing so, the weighted statistics used as sampling weights do not reflect the total population of all 30 villages surveyed. Therefore, the client bases of all five MFIs surveyed plus the total of non-insured households listed by the respective CBOs represents the underlying population of our estimations.

79 To test for potential problems of multicollinearity, we computed the pairwise correlations between the explanatory variables. For the correlation matrix of the explanatory variables, we see no reason for concern.

80 We calculated the variance inflation factors using the *collin* command in Stata. Except for the regressors "age" and "age squared", all VIFs were less than 4.2, so that we see no reason for concern.

exposure as a continuous variable[81], and risk exposure dummies, as well as religious and regional dummies.

3.4.2. Method

There are two ways to specify the econometric model for a household's decision to purchase insurance and its respective coverage including the premium amount. First, it can be modelled as a discrete choice via a probit model, so we estimate as follows:

$$Y_i = X_i^{'}\beta + \varepsilon_i \tag{1}$$

where the binary variable Y_i takes the value of 1 if the household participates in micro life insurance, and 0 otherwise, and X_i refers to the households and respective individual characteristics of the policy holder in our sample.

Second, and more important for the specification of our model, is the fact that a large part of the households surveyed does not purchase insurance, so that the distribution of life insurance premium amount is a mixture of discrete and continuous distribution. There are a variety of models that are able to account for this combined form of distribution. One option is to use a two-part selection model where we first estimate the insurance participation decision using a probit model and subsequently the decision of insurance coverage, i.e. how much to insure using ordinary least squares (OLS), with a sample correction bias term (Heckman 1990). This type of model has the advantage of allowing the likelihood of insurance participation to be determined by variables different from the ones driving the fraction of income paid as insurance premium amount. However, the results of such models are often sensitive to identification exclusions, because it is difficult to identify variables that affect the decision of insurance participation, while not also influencing the insurance coverage. We calculate such models, but find that they are inappropriate, as the sample correction bias term is not significantly different from zero[82].

81 The index is constructed from four questions related to the household's self-perception of its exposure to risks. See for more details, **Essay 2**, Section 2.5 and Table B. 2 (in Appendix B).

82 Besides, the estimates and the levels of significance are different from the one-stage regressions.

Therefore, we assume that a household's life insurance participation decision is a one-stage process and estimate a tobit maximum likelihood[83], as Equation (2) shows, as:

$$Y_i^* = X_i'\beta + \varepsilon_i \text{ with } Y_i = \max(0, Y_i^*) \text{ and } \varepsilon_i \sim N(0, \sigma^2) \quad (2)$$

where Y_i is the income fraction which is paid for insurance coverage to the micro life insurance provider, and X_i is the vector of explanatory variables.

A one-stage process is correct if the household simultaneously decides to purchase insurance depending on what amount of premium the household is able to pay to be covered under the insurance scheme. The likelihood of life insurance uptake and the decision for the insurance coverage shown by the pre-premium amount paid are closely related, and the appropriateness of a tobit model[84] is examined by comparing the signs and magnitudes of explanatory variables that are significantly different from zero to those in the probit model (Amuedo-Dorantes and Pozo 2006). However, it is difficult to conceive of variables that can identify a household's insurance participation decision, without identifying the amount of the insurance premium.

3.5 Findings

3.5.1. Descriptive Statistics

In relation to the dependent variables we present summary statistics for the sample in Table 3.2, divided into the means of each explanatory variable for the full sample, for life insurance buyers and non-buyers[85]. The data set in general and especially the demographic and wealth data confirm that the sample consists of poor and middle-income households. Insurance buyers in general as well as life insurance buyers have a significantly higher asset endowment than non-buyers, so that life insurance buyers are generally better off households in the communities surveyed. Around 20 percent of the household heads have no

---

83 An OLS regression would here result in biased and inconsistent estimates, since life insurance premiums are left-censored at zero (Greene 2003). We estimate life insurance premiums with OLS and find that the estimates and the levels of significance of the estimates are different or respectively lower than in the probit and tobit models.

84 We do not have sufficient statistics that allow for unobserved heterogeneity to be conditional out of the cumulative distribution function, and, thus, the tobit model can only be estimated using random effects.

85 The summary statistics for insurance buyers and non-buyers are presented in Table C. 2 (in Appendix C).

formal education or only primary education, whereas 40 percent of household heads surveyed have secondary education.

Table 3.2: Summary Statistics: Life Insurance Buyers vs. Non-Buyers

Variable	**Full Sample**		**Life Insurance Buyers**		**Life Insurance Non-buyers**	
	Mean	Std. error	Mean	Std. error	Mean	Std. error
Female head	0.169	0.021	0.148	0.029	0.186	0.028
Dependents	2.633	0.074	2.754	0.124	2.543	0.089
Children	1.015	0.058	1.063	0.091	0.979	0.075
Old dependents	1.618	0.065	1.690	0.105	1.564	0.083
Married	0.861	0.019	0.880	0.027	0.846	0.026
Age	47.88	0.644	48.23	0.973	47.61	0.861
Age squared	2428.7	64.5	2,459.9	96.77	2405.01	86.56
No or only primary education	0.191	0.021	0.183	0.033	0.197	0.029
Secondary education	0.409	0.027	0.408	0.041	0.409	0.036
Head is self-employed	0.594	0.027	0.648	0.040	0.553	0.036
Head is unemployed	0.221	0.023	0.218	0.035	0.223	0.030
Asset index	-1.9e-09	0.055	0.180	0.083	-0.136	0.072
Quintile 1	0.2	0.022	0.148	0.029	0.239	0.031
Quintile 2	0.2	0.022	0.176	0.032	0.218	0.030
Quintile 3	0.2	0.022	0.211	0.034	0.191	0.029
Quintile 4	0.2	0.022	0.190	0.033	0.207	0.029
Land ownership	0.773	0.023	0.845	0.030	0.718	0.032
Household's self-perception of risk	9.9e-09	0.168	-0.054	0.073	0.041	0.079
Experienced death of a household member	0.073	0.014	0.070	0.012	0.074	0.019
Experienced severe illness of a household member	0.142	0.019	0.190	0.033	0.106	0.023
Experienced other severe (catastrophic) event	0.336	0.026	0.373	0.041	0.309	0.033
Distance to road	299.52	36.85	351.8	64.47	260.02	42.52
Head is Buddhist	0.903	0.016	0.894	0.026	0.909	0.021
Head is Hindu	0.054	0.013	0.042	0.017	0.064	0.018
Observations	330		142		188	

Source: Authors' calculation.

There are distinct differences between the characteristics of buyers and non-buyers of life insurance. On average, we find that life insurance buyers have significantly more dependents, namely children and old dependents, within their households than non-life insurance buyers. A higher share of household heads with life insurance is married compared to their non-insured counterparts. Moreover, the variable age of household heads shows that the age of household heads who purchase a life insurance policy is significantly higher than the age of household heads who do not. The share of Buddhist and Hindu households is higher among the non-insured as compared to the insured households. The buyers of life insurance report higher self-perception of risk scores than the households in the non-buyers category. This may indicate that life insurance buyers perceive themselves as being more highly exposed to risks than their non-life insured counterparts, thus indicating a higher degree of risk aversion. The "household's self-perception of risks" variable is negatively correlated with the socioeconomic status of the household, i.e. the asset endowment. This could imply that the degree of risk aversion decreases with the rising asset endowment of the household.

We asked each household head who purchased any insurance to provide the main reason for their decision for insurance uptake. Table 3.3 presents the frequencies and percentages for the main reason cited by households for taking up insurance, and especially for life insurance uptake. In the case of insurance uptake, households emphasize the security and especially the risk-reducing effects of insurance. "To secure against future shocks" is the most common and "To protect my family in case of illness/death" the third most self-reported reason. Responses also display other main reasons for insurance uptake, which are not related to risk-reducing benefits, such as "Other", "To obtain collateral for a loan" and "For investment". These categories represent investment and income generating motives underlying the households' decisions to purchase insurance. "Good experiences among relatives and friends" plays only a minor role, indicating the greater importance of security and risk-reducing effects than those of the embedding in social networks such as recommendations from neighbours.

The most popular reason among life insurance purchasers is "To secure against future shocks", followed by "To protect family in case of illness/death". In addition, 6.5% of the households report that they purchased life insurance to cover funeral expenses. Representing more than three quarter of the households' self-reported explanations for life insurance uptake, these responses emphasize the capacity of life insurance to reduce risk and promote security as an ex ante risk coping mechanism. Investment motives are more important, while income generating motives, such as "To obtain collateral for a loan", are reported as less so, for life insurance purchase as compared to the overall insurance purchase mentioned above. It appears that social network and learning effects can be neglected as significant factors in a household's self-reported explanation for life insurance purchase.

Table 3.3: Self-Reported Reason to Purchase Insurance[86]

Why did the household purchase insurance?	Frequency	Percent
To secure against future shocks	180	49.5%
To obtain collateral for a loan	42	11.5%
To protect family in case of illness/death	40	11.0%
For investment	21	5.8%
To finance funeral expenses	13	3.6%
Good experience among relatives and friends	2	0.5%
Other	66	18.1%
Total	**364**	**100%**

Why did the household purchase life insurance?	Frequency	Percent
To secure against future shocks	104	56.5%
To protect family in case of illness/death	27	14.7%
For investment	13	7.1%
To finance funeral expenses	12	6.5%
To obtain collateral for a loan	3	1.6%
Good experience among relatives and friends	1	0.5%
Other	24	13.0%
Total	**184**	**100%**

Source: Authors' calculation.

86 Households surveyed who had purchased any type of insurance were asked to name the main reason for contracting insurance. There are several households who purchased more than one insurance policy, so the frequencies below show the main reason for each policy purchased by the household. Responses were classified into the categories listed in the table. The non-insured households were not asked to name the reasons for not buying insurance.

As we only ask for the main reason for a household's decision to purchase insurance, social network and learning effects may also play a key role in insurance and life insurance uptake, but are not seen as the main reason for it.

Many of these qualitative responses match well with the theoretical models of life insurance participation and their hypotheses, for instance the degree of risk-reduction and of basis risk. However, two reported explanations are inconsistent with theoretical propositions. First, a significant proportion of insurance purchasers cite investment motives as the main reason for insurance uptake. Second, the results indicate that a significant proportion of households purchase insurance only as collateral in order to receive a loan from the respective MFI.

3.5.2. Multivariate Analysis of Micro Life Insurance Participation

The estimates of the probit regression model of micro life insurance participation are presented in Table 3.4[87], where the coefficients are normalized to reflect the marginal effect of a one-unit change in the explanatory variable on the probability of life insurance uptake[88]. Additionally, we use the fractions of income paid for life insurance, i.e. the premium amount, in absolute terms, and after a lognormal[89] transformation, as dependent variables for the estimation of the insurance coverage in two specifications of a tobit model (Table 3.5)[90]. We add further specifications of covariates in Table 3.6 including one specification using the number of dependents instead of the differentiation between young and old dependents, one specification with young dependents only, and one with asset quintiles instead of the asset endowment index. Furthermore, we argue that several household heads without life insurance are older in age, so that either

87 Any causality of the estimation outcomes due to the inability to control for heterogeneity or potential reverse causal relationships is treated cautiously. It is important to note that our findings include potential endogeneity problems, as omitted explanatory or third factor variables also influence the outcomes and explanations shown here. Further, we estimate as well a probit regression model on insurance participation: see the results in Table C. 3 (in Appendix C).

88 We calculated the marginal effects for the probit estimation using the *margeff* command in Stata (Bartus 2005). Average marginal effects and standard errors for marginal effects are calculated using the delta method.

89 The tobit model relies on normality, but respective data are often better modelled as lognormal (Cameron and Trivedi 2009: 531). Therefore, we apply a lognormal transformation to the dependent variable to increase compatibility with a tobit estimation.

90 All coefficients are normalized to reflect the marginal effect of a one-unit change in the explanatory variable on the probability of life insurance uptake.

they are no longer applicable for the purchase of a micro life insurance, or the insurance has already been cashed out due to maturity. In order to test whether that fact has a significant impact on the regressions result, we present estimation outputs for all ages and for a subsample of household heads less than 65 years of age. Whenever necessary, we consider differing results of these samples.

Regarding the proxies for a possible bequest motive discussed earlier, we find very clear support for the hypothesis of the benchmark model, namely that micro life insurance participation is positively associated with a higher number of young dependents in the household (Table 3.4). This turns out to be an economically and statistically significant predictor, indicating an intended bequest motive in micro life insurance participation, which can be altruistic (Tomes 1982), strategic (Bernheim 1991) or even, indeed, unintended, due to precautionary motives, i.e. uncertain lifetime or imperfect insurance markets (Vidal-Meliá and Lejárraga-Garcia 2005).

The majority of micro life insurances in our survey data stress the mortality coverage, which offers benefits for the beneficiaries left behind, i.e. the spouse and the children, and provides only savings or investment options as additional or voluntary components. Therefore, we argue that a policy holder contracts micro life insurance to secure its beneficiaries for the consequences of his/her premature death; this represents an intended bequest motive. In fact, we also find in the other specifications (Table 3.6) of the probit model and for the life insurance consumption in both tobit regression models (Table 3.5), that the probability of purchasing micro life insurance and the extent of life insurance coverage increases with an increased number of children. The same is true for the number of all dependents, which is statistically significant for the subsample of household heads under age 65.

We find, in line with the expectations from the benchmark model, that a household with a higher number of old dependents is marginally less likely to take up micro life insurance and to pay larger sums of micro life insurance premiums, but the outcome is not statistically significant. The marriage status of the head is positively associated with micro life insurance participation and life insurance premiums, giving the impression that these are held for bequest motives, but none of the outcomes is statistically significant.

Table 3.4: Estimates of Probit Regression Model of Life Insurance Uptake

Variable	**Life Insurance Participation All Age Groups**		**Life Insurance Participation Under 65 years only**	
	MEs	**z-stat.**	**MEs**	**z-stat.**
Female Head	-0.0004	-0.31	0.0011	0.39
Children	0.0019	2.99***	0.0019	2.94***
Old dependents	-0.0001	-0.32	0.0003	0.65
Married	0.0007	0.52	0.0005	0.31
Age	-0.0008	-2.13**	-0.0004	-0.87
Age squared	7.9e-06	2.10**	3.26e-06	0.67
No or only primary education	0.1012	1.68*	0.1056	1.48
Secondary education	0.0043	1.83*	0.0039	1.71*
Head is self-employed	0.0035	1.86*	0.0028	1.74*
Head is unemployed	0.0027	0.87	0.0034	0.86
Asset index	0.0039	3.15***	0.0038	2.98***
Land ownership	0.0021	2.40**	0.0021	2.49***
Household's self-perception of risk	-0.00008	-0.21	-0.0002	-0.43
Experienced death a household member	0.0031	0.46	0.0026	0.43
Experienced severe illness a household member	0.00004	0.03	-0.0004	-0.41
Experienced other severe (catastrophic) event	-0.0036	-1.56	-0.0051	-1.65*
Market access: distance to road	3.02e-07	0.26	2.8e-07	0.25
Head is Buddhist	-0.0213	-0.43	-0.0181	-0.39
Head is Hindu	-0.0010	-2.82***	-0.0009	-2.60***
Regional dummies	Yes	-	Yes	-
Observations	330		301	

Source: Authors' Calculation.

Note: For the probit model coefficients are normalized to display marginal effects (MEs). Regression also includes regional dummy variables (outcome omitted). * significant at 10%, ** significant at 5%, *** significant at 1%.

We find, in contrast to the model's prediction, that households who perceived themselves as being more exposed to risk, are less likely to take up life insurance and are negatively related to life insurance coverage, but the value of the marginal effect is lower compared to the uptake of any form of insurance at all and is not statistically significant (Table C. 3 in Appendix C)[91]. Our deviating result might be due to a marginally higher willingness to pay for life insurance of the poor, as they are the most risk averse households due to their high risk exposure (Ray 1999). As the insured are better off than the non-insured in our data set, we suggest that the self-perception of risk exposure of the insured may be higher due to a lower asset endowment, as compared to the non-insured. Therefore, the poor are less able to afford the life insurance premiums and so have no access to the life insurance market.

In terms of religious inclination, our results suggest that household heads who are Hindu or Buddhist are less likely to use life insurance and less able to pay life premiums than Christian household heads, although the results are only statistically significant for the Hindu heads. In fact, life insurance coverage, i.e. the premium amounts, are negatively associated with Hindu headship of a household. We suggest that religious inclination may affect the individual's risk aversion and their attitude towards the institutional arrangements of insurance, especially life insurance. It is important to note that the Hindu households mainly belong to the Ethnic Tamil of Sri Lankan origin, who are mainly located in the Northern and North-Eastern provinces of Sri Lanka. Therefore, the estimated relationship between Hindu headship and micro life insurance participation may also be related to ethnic affiliation. This could imply that, in our sample, it is especially Hindu household heads from the Ethnic Tamil group who are more risk averse or have lower trust in the insurance providing institutions and therefore are less likely to participate in an insurance scheme. However, our results indicate that the access to life insurance may be limited in this case for this group due to discrimination for religious or ethnic reasons by the providing institutions, voluntary self-exclusion for religious reasons or a lower outreach of the MFIs in the Northern regions.

Contrary to the prediction of the Lewis model, but in line with expectations from the contributions on insurance participation in developing countries, we find that households with a higher asset endowment are significantly positively

91 Due to the subjective nature of the households' self-perception of risk exposure, it can function only as an approximate measure of the individual's risk aversion and thus, has limited explanatory power.

associated with life insurance uptake and its respective coverage (Table 3.5)[92]. The same is true for households who own land. In respect to the five asset quintiles which evaluate a household's relative wealth status rank in terms of asset endowment, we find that participation decreases with financial wealth status. The households in the three poorest quintiles are significantly negatively related to micro life insurance participation (Table 3.6) and premium amount. It appears that better off households are less likely to be excluded from the formal insurance, particularly the micro life insurance, market in Sri Lanka. This suggests that the poor have a limited ability to pay the demanded premium amounts for existing micro life insurance schemes.

Furthermore, better off households may have a greater ability to generate income, so that the probability of purchasing life insurance increases with households' income levels. However, it seems plausible that the poor have a lower access to the micro life insurance market than their better off counterparts (Hulme and Mosley 1997, Navajas et al. 2002, Datta 2004), which may be for voluntary or involuntary reasons. Nevertheless, it seems rather unlikely that the poor voluntarily choose not to use micro life insurance.

Our results suggest that household heads with no formal education, or only primary or secondary level, are more likely to use life insurance and to have higher insurance coverage than heads with tertiary education. We find that household heads participating in micro life insurance tend to have lower educational attainment. It seems that households with higher education may neglect micro life insurance participation due to better access to commercial life insurances beyond the microfinance market, reflecting their higher income earning streams. It might be a fact that households with lower educational attainment are especially addressed by micro life insurance providers as the typical microfinance target group, due to their lower and irregular income earning streams. Nevertheless, Lewis (1989) suggests that a higher level of education may increase an individual's risk aversion (Lewis 1989), which might be another explanation for our deviating result. In summary, our outcomes are in contrast to some of the earlier literature, which finds no significant relationship between education and the uptake of insurance, but which additionally controls for financial literacy (Giné et al. 2008, Cole et al. 2009). To understand whether limited financial education about the product limits the participation, it would be necessary to provide additional information on factors related to financial literacy.

92 The same uptake effect is estimated for uptake of any insurance (Table C. 3 in Appendix C).

Table 3.5: Estimates of Tobit Regression Models on Amount of Life Insurance Premiums

Variable	**Tobit**				**Tobit Lognormal**			
	All Age Groups		**Under 65 Years**		**All Age Groups**		**: Under 65 Years**	
	MEs	**z-stat.**	**MEs**	**z-stat.**	**MEs**	**z-stat.**	**MEs**	**z-stat.**
Female head	-177.8	-0.33	177.4	0.29	-0.1306	-0.44	0.1189	0.34
Children	472.0	3.10***	509.6	2.90***	0.3365	4.14***	0.3754	4.13***
Old dependents	-65.26	-0.45	91.27	0.57	-0.0501	-0.55	0.0535	0.53
Married	-28.08	-0.04	-165.2	-0.20	0.0750	0.19	0.0431	0.10
Age	-127.9	-1.57	-54.42	-0.32	-0.1080	-2.23**	-0.0908	-0.95
Age squared	1.12	1.33	0.1648	0.09	0.0010	2.10**	0.0008	0.71
No or only primary education	3449.6	3.36***	3553.8	3.17***	2.0543	4.11***	2.1155	3.77***
Secondary education	1009.2	2.70***	1030.5	2.58***	0.5917	2.89***	0.6045	2.74***
Head is self-employed	742.1	1.91*	691.3	1.73*	0.5574	2.30**	0.5117	2.05**
Head is unemployed	708.0	1.41	688.7	1.16	0.3969	1.34	0.3417	1.03
Asset index	1164.6	4.87***	1233.6	4.89***	0.7556	7.54***	0.8017	7.67***
Land ownership	702.2	2.21**	754.45	2.11**	0.4694	2.41**	0.5340	2.52***
Household's self-perception of risk	-68.73	-0.59	-98.37	-0.74	-0.0231	-0.31	-0.0345	-0.41
Experienced death of a household member	204.7	0.40	142.3	0.27	0.2589	0.78	0.2034	0.60
Experienced severe illness of a household member	323.6	0.86	230.8	0.54	0.0902	0.39	0.0004	0.00
Experienced other severe (catastrophic) event	-682.5	-1.91*	-811.8	-2.14**	-0.4991	-2.17**	-0.6005	-2.43**
Market access: distance to road	0.0837	0.24	0.1244	0.34	0.00002	0.07	0.00006	0.25
Head is Buddhist	-997.5	-1.06	-1130.1	-1.03	-0.8932	-1.31	-0.9424	-1.22
Head is Hindu	-1392.5	-2.98***	-1331.7	-3.17***	-0.8855	-2.96***	-0.8625	-3.08***
Observations	330		301		330		301	

Source: Authors' Calculation.

Note: For the probit model coefficients are normalized to display marginal effects (MEs), for the tobit models the marginal effects for the left-truncated mean are presented. Regression also includes regional dummy variables (outcome omitted). * significant at 10%, ** significant at 5%, *** significant at 1%.

Table 3.6: Estimates of Probit Regression Model of Life Insurance Uptake (Other Specifications)

Variable	All Age Groups MEs	Under 65 Years MEs	All Age Groups MEs	Under 65 Years MEs	All Age Groups MEs	Under 65 Years MEs
Female head	-0.0003	0.0005	-0.0005	0.0013	-0.0018	-0.0007
Dependents	-	-	0.0009	0.0012**	-	-
Children	0.0019***	0.0018***	-	-	0.0016***	0.0016***
Old dependents	-	-	-	-	-0.0006	-0.00009
Married	0.0006	0.0006	-0.0006	-0.0009	-0.0005	-0.00004
Age	-0.0008**	-0.0003	-0.0009**	-0.0003	-0.0008*	-0.0006
Age squared	8.3e-06**	2.6e-06	8.7e-06**	9.3e-07	8.2e-06**	5.9e-06
No or only primary education	0.1007*	0.1074	0.1187*	0.1234	0.0582	0.0560
Secondary education	0.0044*	0.0038*	0.0056*	0.0049*	0.0037	0.0029
Head is self-employed	0.0034*	0.0029*	0.0031*	0.0025	0.0036*	0.0027*
Head is unemployed	0.0024	0.0041	0.0012	0.0027	0.0039	0.0032
Asset index	0.0039***	0.0038***	0.0047***	0.0043***	-	-
Quintile 1	-	-	-	-	-0.0484***	-0.0408***
Quintile 2	-	-	-	-	-0.0142**	-0.0152**
Quintile 3	-	-	-	-	-0.0050***	-0.0046**
Quintile 4	-	-	-	-	-0.0003	0.00003
Land ownership	0.0022**	0.0019***	0.0019**	0.0019**	0.0029***	0.0028***
Household's self-perception of risk	-0.00007	-0.0002	0.00001	-0.0002	0.00003	-0.00004
Experienced death of a household member	0.0029	0.0032	0.0126	0.0078	0.0002	-0.0003
Experienced severe illness of a household member	1.1e-06	-0.0003	0.0013	0.0001	0.0007	-0.00003
Experienced other severe (catastrophic) event	-0.0038	-0.0045	-0.0039	-0.0056	-0.0046	-0.0067
Market access: distance to road	3.6e-07	1.4e-07	8.7e-07	5.8e-07	5.0e-07	5.63e-07
Head is Buddhist	-0.0213	-0.0190	-0.0402	-0.0289	-0.0176	-0.0149
Head is Hindu	-0.0010***	-0.0010***	-0.0012***	-0.0011**	-0.0013***	-0.0011***
Regional dummies	Yes	Yes	Yes	Yes	Yes	Yes
Observations	330	301	330	301	330	301

Source: Authors' Calculation.

Note: For the probit model coefficients are normalized to display marginal effects (MEs). Regression also includes regional dummy variables (outcome omitted). * significant at 10%, ** significant at 5%, *** significant at 1%.

In the following, we emphasize other control variables of the household's decision for life insurance uptake, and of its coverage, which are statistically significant. The likelihood of owning a micro life insurance policy depends in a non-linear way on age, while the age coefficients capture both life cycle and cohort effects. For all empirical evidence reported in this paper, we note that age and cohort effects cannot be separately identified, as we use just a single cross-section of data. In the probit and the tobit regressions with lognormal transformation, we find that the age of the household head is significantly related to life insurance participation and coverage.

In contrast to our expectations, there is no life-cycle effect for life insurance, as participation decreases with age[93]. We argue that, with increasing age, household heads request less life insurance, but from the turning point onwards they request more. One explanation might be that life insurance participation and respective premium amounts are lower for middle aged than for young people. In contrast to the developed country context we suggest that middle aged households are more likely to hold a life insurance policy and with higher face value than their young counterparts (Walliser and Winter 1998). Further, it appears a hump shape of life insurance policy holding, reflecting the change in income over the life cycle, the increase in the number of insurance holders between ages 20 and 40, and the tendency to cash out insurance policies in old age with concomitant lower premium payments. Such a hump shape of life insurance policy holding and also the associated change in income over the life cycle can be rejected for the micro life insurance market in Sri Lanka.

It may be the case that household heads hold less life insurance until middle age, as they are less well educated, less able to understand life insurance and have lower experience with insurance than their younger counterparts. Yet, household heads older than middle age are more likely to request life insurance, due to a higher incentive to protect their family against their premature death, due to their advanced age. However, household heads close to old age – seen as high risk groups by insurers – are also more likely to have limited access to the life insurance market.

Nearly all specifications show that household heads, whether self-employed or contractual workers, are significantly positively associated with micro life insurance participation and its respective insurance coverage. This is possibly due to the fact that micro life insurers and all MFIs in Sri Lanka especially target the self-employed, such as small-scale farmers, even though their activities are mainly associated with lower and more irregular income earning streams.

Beyond this, we control for the incidence of three types of risks, namely for death, illness of a household member – identified as the most severe hazards in

93 The turning point for life insurance participation is 48 years of age in the probit and 60 years of age in the tobit lognormal model.

demand research – and for the experience of any other severe hazard beside these two. Only the experience of another kind of (catastrophic) event appears to be statistically significant, but negatively associated with the participation in and coverage of micro life insurance. This indicates that, after the occurrence of a severe peril, the household is less able to purchase life insurance or extend insurance coverage than without such experience. Possibly, the poor have lower abilities to afford the premiums of a micro life insurance policy after the occurrence of such shock, as they need their financial resources to cover the cost of the peril, income losses and consumption smoothing. Therefore, their access to micro life insurance may be limited. However, we argue that in this case households prefer other risk coping mechanisms, which are more appropriate after the experience of a shock than insurance – namely loans – to cover the direct costs and losses of such an event, so that micro life insurance seems to be substituted by other formally or informally provided risk management strategies.

3.6 Conclusion

The take up rates of microinsurance are still low, whereas the participation in micro life insurance is the highest among the microinsurance products offered. Therefore, it is the objective of this paper to shed more light on the rarely discussed estimates of households' micro life insurance participation in developing countries. Focussing on bequest motives, we primarily evaluate participation patterns and the extent of insurance coverage against a theoretical benchmark model developed by Lewis (1989). We find evidence confirming the model's predictions, but as well results which deviates from the propositions of the model. The study is limited to a single cross section, as it encounters problems in detecting long-term effects. Further research should focus on collecting longitudinal data or conducting randomized experiments to control for unobserved heterogeneity and endogeneity bias.

Using household survey data from Sri Lanka, it appears that correlates of intentional bequest motives (number of young dependents and/or number of dependents) are positively associated with micro life insurance participation, for protection reasons. We view this finding as very strong evidence for the hypothesis that micro life insurance is purchased by low-income households for bequest motives, whereas depending beneficiaries buy micro life insurance to be secure in the event of the premature death of the main breadwinner. Emphasizing the insurance coverage, a tobit model that corrects for the censoring of life insurance premium amounts finds strong effects of the number of children on micro life insurance participation.

In line with empirical findings in the literature, we find that better off households are more likely to participate in a micro life insurance scheme and to pay the respectively small premium sums than their poorer counterparts in Sri Lanka. This supports previous contributions, which suggest that premium payments, even when small, can be unaffordable to many households. It is likely that the amount of the premium becomes a major barrier to any micro life insurance product enrolment, so that the poor may be rationed out of the market altogether. Even though the poor have high incentives to secure against future shocks, their access is still limited. However, in practice most micro life insurers do not have the capacity to extend their provision in the short term, so that one possible solution is for the government to promote the financial and technical assistance for capacity building in the existing MFIs. Furthermore, to improve the social performance of microfinance, it is essential to integrate social performance management, not only as a separate concept, but as an overall performance management in MFIs to target more efficiently the "social bottom line".

However, household heads participating in the micro life insurance schemes tend to have lower educational attainment, while households with higher education have higher access to commercial life insurance schemes, a higher individual risk aversion in respect of their higher educational attainment (Lewis 1989) and typically do not belong to the microfinance target group. Household heads who are self-employed or contractual workers, forming one typical target group, are positively related to micro life insurance participation and related insurance coverage. Deviating from the theoretical model, we find no life-cycle effect for micro life insurance. Until middle age, household heads hold fewer micro life insurance policies, as they seem to be less educated, less able to understand and have less experience with insurance products and markets than their younger counterparts in Sri Lanka.

Interestingly, we find indicative evidence that religious inclination is associated with the participation in micro life insurance schemes in Sri Lanka. Hindu household heads who are mainly affiliated with the Ethnic Tamil group of Sri Lanka origin, are negatively associated with the uptake of micro life insurance. On the one hand, religious inclination may affect the individual's risk aversion, attitude towards life insurance and trust in the provider. On the other hand, religious beliefs in particular may influence a household's attitude towards the afterlife, which may hinder the probability of participating in micro life insurance and lead to voluntary self-exclusion of the poor for religious reasons. It is also plausible that certain religious or ethnic groups have no or only limited access to micro life insurance due to discrimination by the providing institutions, the employed staff or a lower microfinance outreach in their tial area.

Most notably, the government's and donor's support of micro life insurance participation is important in order to serve low-income groups with preventive risk coping strategies. Therefore, it is necessary to emphasize these intentional bequest motives in the marketing measures of such insurance schemes and avoid mixing these with investment motives or misleading offers, such as the promise to use insurance as collateral for loans. From a generic perspective, the government and the microfinance sector has first to take the challenge to improve a household's knowledge about life insurance, so that the poor are more aware about possible life insurance offers and are then more likely to purchase micro life insurance.

Another key factor is building trust in the providers by offering simple, affordable and easily understandable micro life insurance policies. Insurance managers need to promote insurance to potential members, not only using marketing events, but also financial education, especially insurance related seminars. In addition, it may help to address self-exclusion and combat discrimination due to religious beliefs, ethnic affilitation or old age, by improving financial education on insurance and the understanding of the benefits of insurance among such groups before contracting insurance.

Essay 4

4. Microfinance, Micro Life and Health Insurance Enrolment of the Poor in Sri lanka

Abstract:

Microinsurance is an emerging and promising approach for protecting households from the potentially catastrophic expenditures associated with family related shocks. This paper is the first to present and analyse the sequential steps of a household's decision to participate in microinsurance. First, we estimate the determinants of microinsurance participation which is conditional on a household's MFI enrolment, using probit models of household survey data from Sri Lanka. Second, we employ multivariate probit regressions to analyse factors affecting participation in different types of insurance. We find that the household's experience of a family related shock is positively associated with its participation in the micro health insurance schemes under study. There is strong evidence that neither micro life nor micro health insurance has succeeded in proportionately reaching the most vulnerable households in Sri Lanka. Notably, the education level of the household head appears to be a strong determinant of microinsurance participation.

4.1 Introduction

Few recent ideas have generated as much hope for alleviating poverty of poor households in developing countries as the idea of microfinance. In recent years, microfinance has grown and become more and more diversified, due to a higher demand orientation. Taking the demand of low-income groups into consideration has led the microfinance industry to diversify its products into savings and more recently insurance products (Zeller and Sharma 2002, Armendáriz and Morduch 2005). This evolution of microinsurance brings the prospect of reducing the vulnerability of poor people to negative shocks and the consequences of these on income and consumption.

The type of risks faced by the poor, such as those of death, illness, injury and accident, are no different from those faced by others, but the poor are significantly more exposed to family related risks that can severely affect their livelihoods, due to their economic status, and lower income and earning abilities (Holzmann and Joergensen 2000, Siegel et al. 2001). A household can cope with risk at two stages, ex ante and ex post of the occurrence of such shock (Morduch 1995, Townsend 1995, Kazianga and Udry 2006). First, households can smooth income by diversifying economic activities and choosing traditional production or employment activities to protect the households from the consequences of shocks before they occur. Second, households can smooth consumption by borrowing, saving, depleting and accumulating non-financial assets, changing labour supply, or by using formal and informal insurance arrangements to cover the costs after the incidence of a shock. Therefore, the availability of sufficient and efficient risk coping mechanisms are widely seen as an important factor to any poverty reduction strategy.

In the past, insurance was not considered to be an option as an ex ante risk mitigation strategy for low-income groups, as the poor were seen as unable to afford insurance premiums and as uninsurable because of the wide variety of their risk exposure (Siegel et al. 2001). This understanding dramatically changed after the emergence of microinsurance, which is commonly defined as the "protection of low-income people against specific perils in exchange for regular premium payments proportionate to the likelihood and cost of the risk involved" (Churchill 2006: 12). Using risk pooling in return for regular affordable premium payments proportionate to the likelihood and cost of the risk involved, microinsurance policies respond to the limited and variable cash flow of low-income households, and their often unstable economic environment.

In the literature, quantitative studies on micro health (e.g. Asfaw 2003, Jütting 2003, Bhat and Jain 2006, Hamid et al. 2010, Ito and Kono 2010), micro life (e.g. **Essay 1** and **Essay 3**), and on weather or agricultural related microinsurance as rainfall insurance (e.g. Giné et al. 2008, Giné and Yang 2009, Cole et al. 2009) have recently appeared to identify determinants of insurance participation in developing countries[94]. However, none of these studies, as we do, analyses the various sequential steps of the household's insurance participation decision. Moreover, the joint analysis of different types of insurance has received rather limited attention in the academic literature. Therefore, our main objective is to emphasize these sequential steps in a household's decision to participate in different types of microinsurance.

By doing so, we first estimate conditional probit models that account for the first two steps of the insurance participation decision, i.e. what determines the enrolment of a household in an MFI and what are the determining factors of a household's insurance participation which is conditional on the household's

94 The paper is related to another thread of literature, i.e. the growing body of research emphasizing the household's ability to draw on their savings or their entering into informal risk sharing arrangements in order to smooth consumption. Various empirical studies show that households are able to protect consumption against certain income risks in developing countries, but not yet to achieve full insurance so far (See, for example, Townsend 1995, Morduch 1995, Dercon 2002, Kurosaki and Fafchamps 2002, Fafchamps and Lund 2003). We cannot provide a full review of this extensive literature here.

MFI membership. Microinsurance has emerged out of the microfinance sector and can be understood as an extension and adjustment of the microcredit approach to insurance. Several linkages still exist to existing microfinance programmes and institutions worldwide (Siegel et al. 2001), so that we find that microinsurance is mainly offered through existing MFIs, especially in Sri Lanka. Households which purchase insurance may have unobservable characteristics because of their MFI membership, which – we argue – makes them more likely to have access to and also participate in such insurance schemes. Such characteristics might be such things as an informational advantage, higher financial literacy, higher trust in microfinancial services and institutions due to their previous experience with these kinds of institution and products compared to non-members (**Essay 1**, Section 1.1). Furthermore, it is also possible that a household's membership of an MFI might reduce the likelihood of the household's participation in insurance, as other financial services, for instance savings, might be employed as insurance substitutes to protect against the occurrence of certain hazards.

Second, to date there has been very little research on the joint decision making processes of participation in different types of microinsurance (see **Essay 1**, Table A. 4 in Appendix A). Thus, we employ multivariate probit regressions to estimate what affects a household's decision to take up micro life, health or any other type of microinsurance. There are several households which use more than one form of insurance in our data set, so that a household's choice of microinsurance might be influenced by the availability of the different types of microinsurance. And finally, to our knowledge, we are the first to analyse micro life, health and other forms of insurance participation in Sri Lanka. Based on a comprehensive household survey of 330 households from Sri Lanka, we interpret the estimation results concerning the actual usage of microinsurance, i.e. the access to insurance on the supply side and as well on the demand side (World Bank, 2008).

We find some evidence consistent with our expectations. A household's experience of a family related shock – for instance the death of a household member – is positively associated with its participation in the micro health insurance schemes under investigation. Further, there is strong evidence that micro life and health insurance have not yet succeeded in proportionately reaching the most vulnerable households in Sri Lanka. In fact, the poor are less likely to become a member of a respective MFI and are more likely to be excluded from microinsurance participation in Sri Lanka, even if they are a member of an MFI. Education of the household head is a strong determinant of a household's MFI enrolment and microinsurance participation. Finally, larger households are less likely to be enrolled in an MFI, but, conditional on MFI enrolment, larger households are more likely to participate in micro life and/or other microinsurance schemes in Sri Lanka.

The outline of the paper is as follows: Section 4.2 presents the promise of micro life and health insurance, and their possible insurability in Sri Lanka. Section 4.3 provides our conceptual framework, and discusses theoretical and empirical determinants of microinsurance participation and respective propositions in the literature. Section 4.4 presents an overview of the microinsurance market in Sri Lanka, the research design and estimation methodology. The results of the estimations are discussed in Section 4.5. Section 4.6 concludes.

4.2 The Promise of Micro Life and Health Insurance

A high potential of microinsurance, especially of health and life insurance, is identified as a way of reducing family related vulnerabilities of low-income households in developing countries. Microinsurance provides options to overcome the inability to use ex ante preventive risk management strategies or the lack of access to methods to secure against specific perils sufficiently (Loewe et al. 2001, Cohen et al. 2005, McCord et al. 2006). Another motive for microinsurance provision is that insurance markets are still incomplete in developing countries, so that the poor are, in the main, excluded from existing formal insurance schemes. On the demand side, this is constrained by the limited access, abilities and empowerment of the poor to enter the formal insurance markets and, on the supply side, most of the formal insurers are not interested in market segments outside the mainstream formal economy. Hence, the poor depend highly on very costly and mostly insufficient traditional informal coping mechanisms and public social security systems, which are unable to adequately smooth consumption (Townsend 1995, Siegel et al. 2001).

However, microinsurance may play a key role as a possible option or additional element of an integrated social risk management strategy (Siegel et al. 2001). Siegel et al. (2001) suggest that vulnerability can be separated into three components of a "risk chain". First, there is the incidence of the shock or several shocks simultaneously. Second, after the occurrence of the shock the household selects the risk management strategies to respond to the consequences of the peril and third, there is the outcome of the catastrophic event, in terms of a welfare loss. If the shock experienced has led to a loss of household's income, then the household's vulnerability comes from risks (Siegel et al. 2001).

The risks households are faced by can be classified using a number of factors: idiosyncratic or covariate, low- or high-loss, single or repeated events, and combinations of the three previous categories (Siegel et al. 2001). The financial viability of insurance and whether a risk can be covered by an insurance policy depends to a large extent on the type and characteristics of the risk. It is obvious that some risks are insurable, while others are not. Siegel et al. (2001) define three criteria for the "ideal risk", which may be suitable for economic protection and coverage under a private insurance scheme. The most important criteria are "that: a) the risk must be randomly and independently distributed among insured clients, b) risks and losses of insured clients should be determinable, measurable and not catastrophic, and c) the risk and loss should be not influenced by the actions of insured clients" (Siegel et al. 2001: 9). In developing countries, households and individuals are faced by risks that threaten their lives, health, and property from day to day. Low-income households are more affected by these risks, as they are more vulnerable and lack adequate means to manage or minimise their exposure to risk.

Although insurance markets are growing in the developing world (Giné et al. 2008), the global outreach of microinsurance products is so far very limited. Micro life insurance products are identified as the most widely provided microinsurance, but with only 67.2 million people covered so far by life insurance in Asia. Nevertheless, micro health insurance is seen as the most demanded insurance policy around the world (Roth et al. 2007). It is obvious that these new products are established with varying degrees of success. However, microinsurance could cover a wide range of different types of risks, including illness, death, disability and property loss or damage – in fact any risk which can be insurable.

As a new option for low-income households, micro life or health insurance provides a payout in the case of the death of the breadwinner/policy holder or the illness of a household member covered by the insurance. Microinsurance – as a form of low-cost health insurance based on a community, cooperative, or mutual, self-help arrangement – besides financial protection for the poor, can also improve access to health care. Nevertheless, in low-income countries, out-of-pocket payments remain so far the principal means of financing health care, so that out-of-pocket payments for care in relation to an experienced hazard, such as payments for hospitalization or surgery, can push entire households into poverty.

Microinsurance payoffs have to be correlated with the household's income and consumption, so that the risk exposure of the households, especially the risks with the expected highest impact on household income and consumption, are crucial in identifying possible insurable risks in Sri Lanka. We ask the households surveyed to list the most important, second most important and third most important sources of risk that they faced in the following five years (self reported rankings presented in Table 2.1, **Essay 2**)[95]. We find that households report war and terrorism (19%), which explicitly includes the fear of death or injury to the family due to an act of violence, as the most important future peril. It appears that a dramatic increase in input prices (18%) and the serious illness of a working adult household member (8%) are cited second and third most frequently. Environmental or weather related shocks such as drought (8%) follow with the same or floods (1%) and economic shocks such as the loss of a job (5%) with significantly lower frequency. Other important family related shocks such as the death or disablement of a working adult or other household member are reported only in small proportion of the households.

From this, we argue that family related shocks are key risks faced by households in Sri Lanka, as a high share cites war and terrorism, which are related to a fear of family related hazards, and the serious illness of a working adult household member as important future risks. Yet, the death of any household member is marginally reported as an important peril for the household. However, in terms of severity, the death or severe illness of any household member, or an accident or illness leading to permanent disability are in general seen as those risks that have the highest financial impact on household's income and consumption. Family related shocks are generally characterized by their low frequency and thus, they are eligible and suitable for insurance under a microinsurance scheme.

Risks with higher frequency and impact such as less serious health problems are harder to insure, as they are predictable and repetitive events. Aggregate or covariate shocks such as weather related risks, like drought or flood, are harder to insure or the insurance may be limited (Townsend 1995). Due to the limited depth of the resource pool of vulnerable households, existing microinsurance programmes have so far covered only a limited range of risks (Siegel et al. 2001). Overall, idiosyncratic, low loss and single event types of risk, which are mostly represented by the family related shocks in the case of Sri Lanka, are most suitable for insurance under a form of micro life or health insurance scheme (Siegel et al. 2001).

95 For this, the data comes from the household survey conducted with 330 households surveyed in Sri Lanka in 2008. The survey was undertaken for a research project on the demand for microinsurance among low-income households for South Asia.

4.3 A Conceptual Framework of Microinsurance Participation

Two theoretical models are most closely related to the various types of insurance in our study: (1) the standard full information neoclassical model from Ginè et al. (2008) applied on a household participation in an innovative rainfall insurance in India (see **Essay 1**, Section 1.3) and (2) the model of the demand for life insurance developed by Lewis (1989) (see **Essay 3**, Section 3.3.1).

In a simple scenario Giné et al. (2008) consider a model of insurance participation with symmetric information, which predicts that a household's willingness to pay for an insurance contract (i) increases if the household is more risk averse, (ii) increases with the expected insurance payout, (iii) increases with the size of the insured risks and (iv) decreases with basis risk[96]. The willingness to pay for security depends fundamentally on the degree of risk aversion of the household; conversely, thus, the uptake of insurance increases with the household's risk aversion. However, it is obvious that the uptake rate of microinsurance is still low, so that several households, for various reasons, remain uninsured against significant income risks.

Deviating from the above-described simple full information model, adverse selection and moral hazard are often largely seen as potential explanations for barriers to insurance participation (Akerlof 1970, Rothschild and Stiglitz 1976, Browne and Doerpinghaus 1993, Cawley and Phillipson 1999, Winter 2000, Abbring et al. 2003). Therefore, we consider that private household information influences insurance demand and equilibria, so that models of adverse selection and moral hazard are applicable to the micro life and health insurance contracts studied here. In the case of life or health insurance, the insurance providing institution can not fully determine whether an individual is at high or low risk of death. Although the national life expectancy and health status is public information, to observe these on a case by case basis requires a high and not efficient effort of time, costs and human resources. If the households have differential risks and are not charged a premium equal to the expected marginal cost of insurance, adverse selection then exists in the microinsurance market, which can lead to problems, in practice, in the area of microinsurance.

96 I.e. Increases in the correlation between the insurance payout and the risk that is to be insured, or more generally, the household's consumption risk (Giné et al. 2008). Cole et al. (2009) and **Essay 1** use the model as a benchmark. We cannot control for the prediction in relation to the basis risks, as our data set does not include any index based forms of insurance policies.

Moral hazard may also exist in the setting of microinsurance markets, if the household may live with less caution, risk more after contracting microinsurance, omit precautionary actions and overuse care, while the latter is a major problem, particularly for health insurance (Pauly 2004). **Essay 1** (Section 1.7) finds indication for adverse selection in micro life insurance participation. Further, there is evidence for the prevalence of adverse selection, as households having a higher ratio of sick members are more likely to purchase micro health insurance (Ito and Kono 2010). Adverse selection seems to be one reason, in combination with mistrust in the providers and unfamiliarity with insurance, for low take-up rates, high claim rates and low renewal rates. The providers are faced by difficult challenges to manage the incentive problems and simultaneously to educate the poor. Incentive structures such as solidarity enhancing rules seem to keep individual interests restrained by group interests, whereas co-payment rules may be a strong deterrent to very poor households (Hamid et al. 2010). In line with the literature, we test for the presence of adverse selection in micro life and health insurance participation in Sri Lanka.

To consider arguments from existing theoretical work on the demand for life insurance, we present predictions from the model presented by Lewis (1989), which explicitly includes the preferences of the dependents and beneficiaries. Lewis (1989) posits the demand for life insurance as a maximization problem of the beneficiaries, spouse and offspring of the policy holder. The household's willingness to pay for life insurance will then (i) increase with the probability of the breadwinner's death, (ii) increase with the degree of risk aversion, (iii) increase with the present value of the beneficiaries' consumption, (iv) decrease with the policy loading factor and (v) decrease with the household's wealth (Lewis 1989).

From this model, we derive the outcome that the present value of the beneficiary's consumption increases with the number of dependents within the household (**Essay 3**, Section 3.3.1). A household's micro life insurance participation seems to be associated with the number of dependents, especially young dependents, and the marital status "being married", due to intended bequest motives expressing a "joy-of-giving" motive (Hurd 1987, Hurd 1994, Inkmann and Michaelides 2010). Further, we assume that participation in micro health insurance is positively linked to the household size, as household heads seem to have high incentives to insure the entire household (Dror et al. 2007). In particular, women-led households are more likely to be enrolled in health insurance, reflecting the traditional roles of women as the main health caregivers in the family (Khandker 1998, Chankova et al. 2008), so we control for this as well.

Both underlying models show an association between insurance participation and the degree of risk aversion. In a developed country context, there is evidence for a life-cycle effect of the degree of an individual's risk aversion in life insurance participation, although the latter decreases after a certain amount of wealth, income or age (Barsky et al. 1997). Therefore, it is plausible to assume that better off households have a higher ability and willingness to bear a given amount of risk compared to relatively poor households. For developing countries, there is evidence that risk averse households are less likely to purchase an index-based, agricultural microinsurance (Giné et al. 2008) and that households who feel themselves more exposed to risk are less likely to use micro life insurance (**Essay 1**, Section 1.7). Due to this, it may be the fact that risky households, i.e. the households who feel themselves more exposed to risk, have lower access to insurance. However, development theorists assume the poor to be the most risk averse, so that a given loss can be ruinous for the poor in developing countries (Ray 1999). Moreover, the exposure to shocks has an influence on the usage of insurance, but it differs for the tested risks (**Essay 1** Section 1.7, **Essay 2**, Section 2.7, **Essay 3**, Section 3.5). Thus, we control for both the degree of risk aversion and the previous risk exposure in our analysis.

Several contributions to the academic literature have shown that life insurance participation is positively related to income and wealth, using individual household data both in a developed and developing country context (Lewis 1989, Truett and Truett 1990, Browne and Kim 1993, Outreville 1996). For participation in an index-based, agricultural microinsurance scheme (Giné et al. 2008) and especially for health insurance (Jütting 2003, Pauly 2004, Bhat and Jain 2006, Dror et al. 2007), it is also evident that households in developing countries are more likely to take up insurance with the increasing income or wealth of the household. In contrast to this, Chankova et al. (2008) find no evidence that individuals from the poorest quintiles are more likely to be excluded from mutual health organizations. Evidence for Bangladesh suggests that micro health insurance placement has a significant beneficial effect only on food sufficiency, but not on other poverty indicators (Hamid et al. 2010). Interestingly, Ito and Kono (2010) find that households with sick household heads are less likely to purchase health insurance, as the sickness of the heads reduces the household's income streams and so makes it difficult for the household to finance appropriate insurance premiums. In sum, we expect that micro life and health insurance participation is positively correlated with the income and wealth status of the household.

In principle, a higher level of education is positively correlated with the purchase of any type of insurance product, as it raises a household's ability to understand the benefits of risk management and insurance (McCord 2001, Beck and Webb 2002, Chankova et al. 2008, Giné et al. 2008). Factors relating to financial literacy have a significant impact on an insurance participation decision

(Cole et al. 2009), but we did not collect data to study this issue here. Nevertheless, we expect that more educated heads are more likely to understand insurance, and thus, be more likely than their less educated counterparts to participate in such insurance schemes. It is important to note that education has an increasing effect on the length of dependency and so on the participation in forms of micro life insurance which offer the extension of mortality coverage for the breadwinner. In the case of micro health insurance, the poor may additionally not only not understand the concept fully, but their medical knowledge is also often poor, and it is difficult for them to understand what is and what is not covered under the policy (Chankova et al. 2008, Ito and Kono 2010).

Another important aspect in the microinsurance participation of low-income households is the trust of the clients towards the providers (Cole et al. 2009). Participation in village networks, familiarity with the insurance vendor or various community-based organisations, and endorsement from a third party are strongly correlated with the decision to participate in an insurance scheme (Schneider 2005, Giné et al. 2008, Chankova et al. 2008, Cole et al. 2009). We expect that factors related to trust significantly determine insurance participation decisions.

4.4 Market Overview, Research Design and Methodology

4.4.1. The Microinsurance Sector in Sri Lanka

The microinsurance market is still an emerging one in Sri Lanka, from both the demand and supply side perspectives (Rajivan 2007, Roth et al. 2007). Even though a significant increase in microinsurance provision is predicted for the coming years, the average penetration of life insurance in Sri Lanka has ranged between 1.4 to 1.6% during the last three years (ADB 2006). One reason for this was the high inflation rates in the past, which have reduced the maturity value of cash-value life insurance policies and so led to public apathy regarding contracting life insurance. This is a dilemma faced by the life insurance business, but is not relevant for the as yet low uptake rates of micro health insurance.

In Table 4.1, we present the main characteristics of the Sri Lankan microinsurance providers which are covered by the underlying analysis[97]. From a historical perspective, the development of microinsurance schemes arose out of

97 In 2006, there were over 14,000 microfinance providers in Sri Lanka, out of which nearly 3,800 belonged, as active outlets, to SANASA (GTZ 2009).

the Mutuals and CBOs, starting with funeral aid society concepts in the 1990s[98]. We find that the five MFIs under examination, the WDF, the WDBF, SANASA, YASIRU and SEEDS served a total of more than 241,800 clients with their microinsurance products in 2008[99]. Contrary to the numbers from the ADB (2006), the number indicates a reasonably high outreach of microinsurance in Sri Lanka[100]. Even though the private insurance market is dominated by private insurance companies, the main providers or distributors of microinsurance contracts are still the unregulated mutuals and NGOs, such as YASIRU and SEEDS (Enarsson and Wirén 2006, Roth et al. 2007). Some of these MFIs retail the products of registered insurance companies, while some have built up and registered their own insurance companies (GTZ 2009).

Table 4.1: Characteristics of Microinsurance Providers in Sri Lanka

General characteristics of microinsurance providers	
Microinsurance schemes	5 Microinsurance providers: WDF, WDBF, SANASA, YASIRU and SEEDS
Types of microinsurance products	Life, death, loan protection, funeral, accident, health, hospitalisation, hospital cash benefits, surgical operations, marriage, childbirth
Group or individual product	Individual, group insurance for funeral assistance
Clients in total[101]	241,800
Enrolment requirements	Above 18 years, but not older than 65 years. Each application is subject to strict underwriting rules
Premium payments on average[102]	0.1 to 4 US$ per month (Enarsson and Wirén 2006, own data)

Source: Authors' illustration.

All microinsurance providers covered in the study encouraged enrolment of the entire household, as a measure to prevent adverse selection, but some providing institutions limit the number of beneficiaries. A wide variety of microinsurance products are provided by these five MFIs, namely health, property, and life insurance, which includes death benefits, which can thus be

98 This concept was invented by ALMAO, the precedessor organisation of SANASA.

99 Since one client can have multiple insurance contracts, the total number of insured clients probably overestimates the client outreach of the respective MFIs.

100 In comparison to the overall population size of more than 20 million people, the outreach of microinsurance is still not sufficient, but succeeds in reaching a reasonable number of households from rural Sri Lanka.

101 For Sri Lanka, the number of clients is from November 2008.

102 US$ at exchange rate at time of survey.

interpreted as a term life insurance, or combined additionally with the death compensation, accident, hospitalization, health and other benefits[103]. Therefore, we argue that the microinsurance product types and portfolios are highly diversified in Sri Lanka, not only because of their high coverage, but as well due to the prevalence of a high number of providing institutions and the long involvement of these actors in the market. Most of the microinsurance policies discussed in this study are based on an individual basis of monthly premiums, with temporary exclusion from the policy benefits for households who do not regularly pay their dues. It appears that the minimum and total premium payment per month is relatively low in Sri Lanka.

4.4.2. Sources of Data, Definition of Variables and Summary Statistics

The data for this study comes from a household survey conducted in Sri Lanka in 2008. The survey is based on a questionnaire which is also used for the study in **Essay 1,** except for some adaptations due to country-specific features. Additional specific objectives of the individual country studies and household sample selection are described in greater detail elsewhere[104].

In total, 330 households were interviewed in 30 villages in Sri Lanka, drawn from two strata of (micro)insured and non-insured households, of which 240 households use and 90 do not use any insurance, including as well insurance policies offered by institutions other than the five respective MFIs. 304 households of the participating household heads are members of, associated with an MFI, and/or at least use a financial service, i.e., all 240 insured households are considered MFI members. Among the insured, 142 households purchased a life insurance policy, 29 households health insurance and 79 households another type of insurance, for instance vehicle insurance[105]. These

103 For instance, YASIRU offers products with coverage of death, accidents and health. The WDF in Hambantota provides special products in addition to death, hospitalization and health products, namely marriage and child birth. ALMAO covers death, disability, hospitalization and life savings.

104 See **Essay 2**, Section 2.5 and **Essay 3**, Section 1.1.3.4.1.

105 We focus on voluntary insurance offers so that compulsory insurance products such as credit life insurance, which is typically linked to the uptake of a loan or any other financial product, are dropped from the analysis. Further, it is important to note that the use of insurance is not exclusive.

insurance purchases are not exclusive, i.e. there are households which use more than one insurance type.

In a first step, we identified the main suppliers of voluntary microinsurance for low-income households in Sri Lanka. Those are the so far mentioned five MFIs, namely WDF, WDBF, SANASA, YASIRU and SEEDS. In a second step, two or three MFIs were selected from each district, except for Vavuniya and Batticaloa. For each district two or three villages were chosen, due to the high density of insured households. In total, we included 30 villages in Sri Lanka, which are at least representative for all villages, in which microinsurance is accessible via the selected MFIs. As microfinance is clearly concentrated in rural areas[106], the underlying survey seems representative for rural villages in Sri Lanka. Third, the insured households in the respective villages were randomly chosen from the client bases of the MFIs surveyed. Fourth, the non-insured households were randomly selected from household lists provided by CBOs located in the villages where the MFIs operate. However, the CBOs selected are not involved in the microfinance activities of the microinsurance provider, but are involved, for instance, in community strengthening, infrastructure, health or economic issues beyond microfinance. The number of insured and non-insured households selected from each village varied from 10 to 15. Fifth, the data collection was based on a household characteristics questionnaire including a special section about the household's integration in financial markets, their enrolment in different financial institutions, and their use of the financial services, i.e. loans, savings and insurance (Zeller and Sharma 2002).

Table D. 1 (in Appendix D) summarizes the definition of the variables in the estimations[107]. We include different household characteristics like demographic and wealth variables, the household head's education level and economic activities, information about remittances received by the household, the household's self-perception of risks, the household's previous risk exposure, and regional dummies. To avoid potential endogeneity problems, we constructed an asset index, which is controlled for so that none of the financial services contracted are used to purchase any asset. The index variable "household's self-perception of risk" is constructed from three questions related to the household's self perception of exposure to health shocks, weather and environ-

106 More than 90 percent of MFI branches are located in rural areas (GTZ 2009).

107 To test for potential problems of multicollinearity, we computed the pairwise correlations between the explanatory variables. For the correlation matrix of the explanatory variables, we see no reason for concern. We calculated the variance inflation factors using the *collin* command in Stata. Except for the regressors "age" and "age squared" all VIFs were less than 2.38 for the survey data (Specification II: 2.58) for Sri Lanka. We see no reason for concern as none of the variance inflation factors was higher than 2.58.

ment related shocks, and economic shocks compared with neighbouring households, and one question about the household's own rating of its willingness to take risks, using factor analysis[108].

Sample characteristics are summarized in the descriptive statistics for insurance participation in Table D. 2 (in Appendix D) and for micro life, health and other insurance participation in Table D. 3 (in Appendix D). The proportion of female households is higher among insurance non-buyers than among insurance buyers, while only 17% of the households are female-headed. The share of female-headed households which participate in micro life or health insurance is even smaller. Insurance buyers for all types of insurance covered typically live in larger households, and among them are slightly more married household heads than among non-buyers. The ratio of ill household members is significantly higher among participants, especially in micro health or any other form of insurance, than among non-participants. Insurance buyers are significantly older than insurance non-buyers. Among the insurance buyers, the households own more land, have more remittance receipts, a lower share of uneducated, only primary or secondary educated household heads and a lower share of self-employed household heads than among the insurance non-buyers. In Sri Lanka, insurance buyers belong to wealthier households as compared with non-buyers[109]. The households which have purchased any of the underlying types of insurance have a significantly higher risk assessment index in Sri Lanka. A higher share of insurance and especially micro health insurance buyers experienced a severe illness of a household member than was the case for non-buyers. The same is true for health insurance users in the case of the experience of any other severe shock.

4.4.3. Methodology

We use econometric analysis to identify the factors affecting the insurance participation decision. The decision to buy insurance can be formulated in two interrelated choices. First, the choice of the household is related to the decision to buy or not buy any insurance. Second, if the household decides to buy insurance, then the second choice is which type of insurance to buy. Furthermore, the household has to define for how many people in the household and for what ex-

108 For more details see **Essay 2**, Section 2.5 and Table B. 2 (in Appendix B).

109 Economic status quintiles were assigned at the household level using the asset endowment index. Table C. 2 (in Appendix C) reflects the households' distribution among quintiles.

tent of coverage the insurance is purchased. When estimating the determinants of insurance uptake based on cross-sectional data, one encounters the important challenge of dealing with both the problems of "endogeneity" and "self selection" (Jütting 2003). Therefore, we treat any implication of a causal relationship with caution and control as far as possible for potential endogeneity issues; thus, for instance, we apply an adjusted asset index. Household heads who self-select the insurance uptake may have unobservable characteristics – related to preference or existing enrolment in an MFI – which make it more likely for them to participate in an insurance scheme (which are mainly offered by such MFIs) and may influence their decision to use insurance (Waters 1999). That is why the two ways of choosing to take up insurance may proceed in three sequential steps.

To control for self-selection, we utilise two binary probit models to estimate the first two sequential steps of the insurance participation decision, i.e. the participation in an insurance scheme conditional on the household's enrolment in an MFI. In the first probit model we estimate the determinants on the whole sample of a household's enrolment in an MFI. We hypothesize that, after controlling for individual, household and regional characteristics, members of an MFI have better access to and are more likely to use insurance than non-members. In the second model, we investigate the effect of the determinants of a household's usage of insurance on the subsample of the households that were members of an MFI, i.e. we examine insurance participation which is conditional on MFI membership. In contrast to **Essay 1**, our analysis is in this way not faced with the problem of limited variance on the supply side, as all provinces and the five major microinsurance providing institutions are covered in the underlying survey.

It is assumed that MFI enrolment or the insurance participation of a household (p) depend on the following factors: the wealth status of the household (w), characteristics of the household head (H), household characteristics (Z), regional characteristics (R) and on the error term u, which is uncovariant with the other regressors. The following equation is applied for both models using the described sample structure:

$$p_i = f(w_i, H_i, Z_i, R, u) \qquad (1)$$

In order to estimate the probability of participation for each equation we use a binary probit model:

$$p_i^* = \beta w_i + \alpha H_i + \phi Z_i + \delta R + u_i \qquad (2)$$

$p_i^* = 1$ if $p_i^* > 0$, meaning the household i is member of an MFI (equation 1) or uses insurance (equation2),

$p_i^* = 0$ otherwise.

For the third step of the insurance participation decision, we apply a trivariate probit model for the use of different types of insurance, i.e. life, health and any other insurance. Since preliminary analyses of our three outcomes of interest revealed that there may be a correlation between the different outcome categories[110] and the use of any insurance is not being exclusive among the households, so that there are households who use more than one insurance type, we assume that households' choices of different types of insurance are interrelated. The trivariate probit model enables us to estimate three dichotomous dependent variables simultaneously and explicitly model the correlation in disturbance terms, using a method of simulated maximum likelihood[111]. Therefore, we use it to estimate the determinants of the three different types of insurance, which is given by:

$$\begin{aligned} L^* &= X'\beta_L + \varepsilon_L \quad L^* = 1 \text{ if } L^* > 0, 0 \text{ otherwise,} \\ H^* &= X'\beta_H + \varepsilon_H \quad H^* = 1 \text{ if } H^* > 0, 0 \text{ otherwise,} \\ O^* &= X'\beta_O + \varepsilon_O \quad O^* = 1 \text{ if } O^* > 0, 0 \text{ otherwise,} \end{aligned} \tag{3}$$

where L^*, H^* and O^* are the true, unobserved propensities to use life insurance, health insurance or any other insurance. The term X′ represents the vector of independent variables, i.e. the socio-demographic control variables. We assume that the distribution of the three outcomes is multivariate normal, i.e.:

$$E[\varepsilon_L] = E[\varepsilon_H] = E[\varepsilon_O] = 0 \quad \text{and} \quad Var[\varepsilon_L] = Var[\varepsilon_H] = Var[\varepsilon_O] = 1 \tag{4}$$

In multivariate probit models the computation of marginal effects is difficult. We therefore calculated the APEs on the marginal probabilities of the independent variables for each equation by averaging sample partial effects[112].

110 Analyses that ignore the correlations across outcomes, such as simple univariate probits, could therefore lead to biased results (Jones 2007). The coefficient estimates from the trivariate probit model account for unobserved correlation among the outcomes and are therefore less biased than those produced by three separate probit models.

111 We use the Stata application *mvprobit,* which uses the Geweke-Hajivassiliou-Keane simulator (Cappellari and Jenkins 2003, Greene 2003, Kis-Katos 2007).

112 We use the Stata application *mvppred* to calculate the predicted probabilities of a positive response for each of the three outcomes (Capellari and Jenkins 2003) and, based on this, we calculate the APEs using the Stata routine *margeff* (Bartus 2005).

4.5 Estimating the Patterns of Microinsurance Participation

4.5.1. Marginal Coefficients for Microfinance Enrolment and Insurance Participation

The estimation outcomes of the first two sequential steps of the microinsurance participation decision, i.e. a household's MFI enrolment and microinsurance participation conditional on MFI membership, estimated using a conditional probit model, are presented in Table 4.2[113]. Two model specifications have been estimated for each dependent variable and estimation: the first one includes, among the other regressors, an asset endowment index as continuous variable and the second uses dummies for asset endowment quintiles. Further, we calculated marginal effects for two reference households: (1) a female-headed household which has eight household members, a household head at age 45 years with no formal or only primary education, but self-employed, with an asset endowment index of zero, without any land, who receives remittances, has an household's self-perception of risk index of one, has experienced a death, an illness of a household member and an additional shock in the past five years, and (2) a male-headed household which has four household members, a head who has attained secondary education, an asset endowment index of two, without any remittances and, for the other variables, the same outcomes as the first reference household[114]. In the following, we highlight our interpretations of the statistically significant associations.

In the literature, female-headed households are generally expected to have relatively lower abilities and resources to enter the microfinance market, as they are commonly assumed to be less wealthy than their male-headed counterparts in developing countries. Interestingly, we find the opposite for Sri Lanka, where female-headed households are significantly more likely to be enrolled in an MFI than male-headed households. This indicates that in the Sri Lankan microfinance sector women are treated as a particular target group by MFIs, such as WDF and WDBF, due to an underlying higher repayment probability which is caused by the use of group loans of socially connected women, and a higher in-

113 We estimate binary probit models for microinsurance use without control for membership of any MFI. We find changes due to the signs and significance levels of the estimation coefficients (Table D. 4 in Appendix D).

114 It is important to note that it may be better to create a benchmark value – a reference case – for which the marginal effects are calculated (Cameron and Trivedi 2009).

centive for women to provide security to their families than male credit ents.

We find that household size is significantly negatively linked with membership in an MFI[115]. In Sri Lanka, the probability decreases for the first reference household by -0.08 and for the second by -0.02. This implies that households with a larger number of dependents have a higher share of consumption in relation to their income, are less able to provide collateral, and thus have limited access to MFIs. However, in line with the Lewis model, household size is significantly positively linked to microinsurance participation. If the household is an MFI member, the access to microinsurance seems not to be limited for households with a higher number of dependents. Indeed, our results imply that larger households may have a higher incentive to use their limited resources to obtain risk-reducing effects, as they are commonly more exposed to family related risks.

The age of the household head is significantly related to microinsurance participation. The turning point is 57[116] years of age, which implies that household heads with increasing age do not request more insurance. One explanation for this outcome may be that older household heads with MFI membership are less educated and thus, less able to understand microinsurance products and markets than their younger counterparts.

In line with our expectations and previous findings, we find that household heads with no formal, only primary or secondary education are less likely to be enrolled in an MFI or participate in the microfinance market than more highly educated heads[117]. This indicates that a higher level of education may raise a household's ability to understand the benefits of risk management, in particular of microfinancial services, and so may increase a household's willingness to become a member of an MFI. We find the opposite for microinsurance uptake which is conditional on a household's MFI enrolment, as no formal, either primary or secondary education is positively correlated with microinsurance uptake. This implies that the commonly identified constraint of poor understanding of insurance products among lower-educated households seems to be relieved if these lower-educated households are MFI members.

115 In the data set, the correlation coefficient shows that household size is highly correlated with the number of dependents (0.79).

116 The turning point is 49 years of age for the specification II.

117 It may be better to use here years of schooling instead of the three educational dummies, but the survey does not include reliable data on that.

Table 4.2: Institution Membership and Microinsurance Participation Conditional on Membership in Sri Lanka

Variable	Membership (I)	Insurance Purchase (II)	Membership (I)	Insurance Purchase (II)
Female head	0.3278***	-0.0021	0.2503***	-0.0069
Household size	-0.0583**	0.0069***	-0.0936***	0.0055**
Age	-0.0482	-0.0036**	-0.0084	-0.0029**
Age squared	0.0003	0.00003*	-0.00007	0.00003**
Education of household head (base: tertiary education)				
No or only primary education	-0.9615***	0.6278***	-0.9692	0.2097
Secondary education	0.0532	0.0118	-0.0172	0.0075
Occupation of household head (base: formal employee/employer)				
Head is self-employed	-0.8374***	0.0125	-0.8161***	0.0098
Head is unemployed	-0.7462***	0.0096	-0.7659*	0.0039
Asset index	0.2132***	0.0171***	-	-
Asset quintiles (base: richest 20%)				
Quintile 1	-	-	-0.9996***	-0.2621***
Quintile 2	-	-	-0.9999***	-0.0251***
Quintile 3	-	-	-0.9984***	-0.0781***
Quintile 4	-	-	-	0.0033
Land ownership	0.2632	-0.0017	0.3424*	0.0046**
Remittance	0.0899*	0.5448	0.0901**	0.6719**
Household's self-perception of risk	0.0028	0.0031**	0.0408	0.0017
Household's risk experience (base: no risk experience)				
Experienced death of a household member	-	0.1648	-	0.0361
Experienced severe illness	-0.1737	-0.0029	-0.1308	-0.0043**
Experienced other severe shock	0.4426***	-0.0422*	0.4806***	-0.0419*
Regional dummies	Yes	Yes	Yes	Yes
Observations	330	304	330	304

Source: Authors' calculation.

Note: Probit model. Coefficients are normalized to display marginal effects (MEs). The asterisks indicate level of significance (Robust z-statistics): ***significant at 1 percent, ** significant at 5 percent, * significant at 10 percent.

According to our results, we confirm earlier contributions that households with a head who is either self-employed or a contractual worker are significantly less likely to obtain membership in an MFI than households with a head who is either regularly employed or an employer. Due to the irregular nature and low level of their incomes, such households seems to have only limited access to the microfinance market. Our results indicate, in line with our expectations and earlier contributions (Hulme and Mosley 1997, Navajas et al. 2002, Datta 2004), that better off households are more likely to become a member of an MFI and thus, to purchase microinsurance in Sri Lanka. For the asset index the probability of being enrolled in an MFI in Sri Lanka for the female-headed reference household increases by 0.297, while for the male-headed reference household it increases by 0.553.

Households from the richest quintile are more likely to participate in microinsurance compared to those from the poorest quintiles (Table 4.2), so the poorest households are not covered by the microinsurance schemes under consideration in Sri Lanka. This may indicate that the poor have reduced accessibility to MFIs and are less likely to take up microinsurance than their better off counterparts.

Deviating from the standard neoclassical model of Giné et al. (2008), we find that households among the MFI members who perceived themselves as being more exposed to risk, are significantly more likely to use microinsurance[118]. This indicates that households may not see insurance as an additional risk which is related to mistrust in the MFI and its staff or to misunderstanding of the offered microinsurance products.

Remittances are highly associated with enrolment in the microfinance market and the use of microinsurance as well. In contradiction to earlier findings from **Essay 1**, Section 1.7, we find a positive association of remittances with microinsurance uptake. This implies that remittances function more as an additional financial resource to take up microinsurance in Sri Lanka. Further, we find for the tested three risk dummies that households who experienced an additional shock are significantly less likely to use microinsurance, whereas the estimates for the experience of death and illness are not statistically significant.

118 However, a household's self-perception of risk exposure can only function as a proxy for the risk aversion of the household. It may give an indication that a higher exposure to risk of a household may represent a higher awareness of the household towards risks and its higher aversion of risks. Due to the subjective measurement of the households' self-perception of risk exposure, it can function only as an approximate measure of the individual's risk aversion and thus, has limited explanatory power.

4.5.2. Multivariate Probit Models on the Type of Insurance Participation

The results of the trivariate probit regressions for the third sequential step of a household's insurance participation decision, i.e. what determines the usage of micro life, health and other forms of insurance, are presented in

Table 4.3 and in Table D. 5 (in Appendix D), showing the APEs of the explanatory variables on the marginal probability of using the different types of insurance. Deviating from the previous estimations, two more explanatory variables – namely married head and the ratio of ill household members – are added here according to the relevance of bequest motives, particularly for micro life, and adverse selection for micro life and health insurance. Similar to the previous estimations, we calculate two specifications.

It is important to note that the three outcome categories, i.e. the types of insurance, are not mutually exclusive. The estimated correlation coefficients, listed at the bottom of the tables, indicate that the residuals of the three outcome categories are correlated. Two of the estimated correlation coefficients are negative and statistically significant for Sri Lanka[119]. The correlation coefficient between the unexplained part of the use of micro life and other insurance amounts to -0.69 and between micro health and other insurance to -0.41, suggesting that there exist unobservable characteristics of the household that influence a household's decision to purchase life or any other form of insurance, and likewise health or any other form of insurance[120]. This outcome shows that, from the household's perspective, the participation in life or any other form of insurance and health or any other form of insurance are conflicting alternatives.

In line with the literature, female-headship of a household is positively associated with the use of micro health insurance in Sri Lanka, which may reflect a higher incentive to provide security, especially health care, to the household compared with male-headed households.

119 Hence, the application of the trivariate probit regression is appropriate for the Sri Lankan case, as the assumption, that the correlations between the error terms of the three equations are all zero, can be rejected at a high significance level (X^2 = 31.439; p = 0.000). However, separate probit estimations for each outcome yield very similar coefficients to those of the multivariate probit model. We find only slight changes due to the signs and significance levels of the estimation coefficients.

120 In the second specification, these correlation coefficients amount to -0.71 and -0.58.

Table 4.3: Multivariate Probit Results on the Type of Insurance for Sri Lanka (I)

Variable	Life Insurance			Health Insurance			Other Insurance		
	Coeff.	**APEs**	**z-stat.**	**Coeff.**	**APEs**	**z-stat.**	**Coeff.**	**APEs**	**z-stat.**
Female head	0.016	0.0003	0.00	1.318	0.0005	1.94**	-0.063	-0.004	-0.11
Household size	0.241	0.049	2.39**	0.234	0.00001	1.24	0.336	0.028	3.33***
Married head	0.056	0.009	0.09	1.322	0.00001	3.12***	-0.906	-0.104	-1.59
Ratio of ill household members	0.335	0.073	0.38	-0.146	-2.99e-06	-0.15	0.077	0.005	0.23
Age	-0.204	-0.032	-3.91***	-0.109	-2.41e-06	-0.87	-0.118	-0.006	-1.74*
Age squared	0.002	0.0003	4.24***	0.001	2.88e-08	0.90	0.0008	0.00005	1.12
Education of household head (base: tertiary education)									
No or only primary education	1.939	0.568	5.02***	3.094	0.031	2.76***	0.079	0.005	0.12
Secondary education	0.958	0.193	5.09***	1.829	0.0005	2.06**	0.197	0.013	0.54
Occupation of household head (base: formal employee/employer)									
Head is self-employed	0.768	0.127	1.69*	-0.811	-0.00005	-1.70*	-0.358	-0.024	-1.35
Head is unemployed	0.332	0.066	0.82	-0.905	-0.00001	-2.37**	-0.439	-0.022	-2.01**
Asset index	1.117	0.338	6.29***	1.460	0.002	3.30***	0.503	0.049	2.71***
Land ownership	0.528	0.079	1.35	-0.335	-0.00001	-0.42	0.062	0.004	0.25
Remittance	0.629	0.154	1.35	-1.467	-8.54e-06	-1.38	1.433	0.259	1.33
Household's self-perception of risk	0.016	0.003	0.08	0.194	8.40e-06	1.18	-0.048	-0.003	-0.26
Household's risk experience (base: no risk experience)									
Experienced death of a household member	0.709	0.177	1.15	1.000	0.0003	3.45***	0.564	0.055	1.52
Experienced severe illness	-0.051	-0.009	-0.11	1.199	0.0004	1.35	-1.206	-0.037	-1.69*
Experienced other severe shock	-0.956	-0.143	-3.18***	0.099	2.97e-06	0.25	-1.185	-0.059	-3.45***
Regional dummies	Yes	-	-	Yes	-	-	Yes	-	-
Est. correlation coeff.	$\rho_{21} = 0.094$	1.04		$\rho_{31} = -0.693$	-9.13***		$\rho_{32} = -0.411$	-3.03***	

Source: Authors' calculation.

Note: Results of the trivariate probit model are estimated by SML with 20 pseudorandom draws. The t-statistics refer to the estimated coefficients and are based on robust standard errors. Average partial effects (APEs) are calculated with respect to the marginal probability of each type of insurance. The model also includes a constant. Sample size is N = 240 observations. The asterisks indicate level of significance: *** significant at 1 percent, ** significant at 5 percent, * significant at 10 percent.

This confirms the fact that women are the main health caregivers in the family due to traditional role models of women; thus, they prioritize more health-related expenditures for the family than men, including the premium paid to a micro health insurance scheme.

From the predictions of the model for life insurance demand, we expected a positive relationship between household size and the participation in micro life insurance due to bequest motives. Indeed, we find a positive association for micro life and any other form of insurance. In our first specification, household size, indicating the number of dependents in the household, is an economically and statistically significant predictor of micro life insurance participation due to an intended bequest motive (Hurd 1987, Hurd 1994).

However, we find no significant relationship between micro life insurance participation and the marriage status of the head as the other possible bequest related determinant. Nevertheless, the outcome shows that being married is significantly positively linked to the uptake of micro health insurance in our first specification and negatively related to the use of any other form of insurance in our second specification. Most notably, married household heads – similar to female-headed households – seem to have a higher propensity to internalize the costs and consequences related to health shocks and related care than unmarried heads.

In contrast to earlier findings in the literature, we find no evidence of the existence of adverse selection or asymmetric information in the microinsurance market, as there is no significant outcome for the ratio of ill household members[121]. Further, our results show no life-cycle effect for any of the three insurance types, which indicates a u-shaped age pattern for Sri Lanka. There is significant evidence for such an age pattern for micro life participation in both and for health insurance participation only in the second specification. It appears that household heads have a decreasing willingness to pay for insurance up to a specific age, before their willingness increases due to higher incentives to protect their families from certain hazards[122].

Deviating from the underlying theoretical model of Lewis and the bulk of the literature, we find that household heads with no formal, only primary or secondary education are significantly more likely to buy life and health insurance than heads with tertiary or higher education in Sri Lanka. This implies that lower educated household heads are not excluded from microinsurance partici-

---

121 We also checked for the explanatory variable "households with a sick household head" and find no significant association.

122 The turning point of the age variable for micro life insurance is 59 years, for health insurance 61 and for any other form of insurance 63.

pation and do not have a lower willingness to pay for it than highly educated heads. In contrast to the findings of Chankova et al. (2008) and Ito and Kono (2010), our results imply that the concept of micro health insurance is also capable of being understood by the less well educated heads. Moreover, we suggest that these households may have lower income earning opportunities, so that they may have higher incentives to secure their families against the negative outcomes of certain shocks, such as death or sickness. Following previous contributions in the literature (Giné et al. 2008, Cole et al. 2009), it would be better to use additional determinants related to financial literacy, especially insurance knowledge, to capture the relationship between the understanding of insurance concepts and the propensity of low-income households to participate in different types of microinsurance schemes (Giné et al. 2008, Cole et al. 2009).

We find that self-employment and unemployment are significantly negatively associated with the use of micro health insurance, and unemployment only with the uptake of any other insurance. Since we do not know much about the specific causality here, it is important to note that both occupational statuses are related to lower income earning possibilities, which indicates a lower ability and willingness to pay for micro health or any other form of insurance.

In line with the benchmark model from Lewis, wealthier households in Sri Lanka, i.e. households with a higher asset endowment, are more likely to use micro life, health or any other form of insurance. Due to the fact that households from the poorest quintile are significantly less likely to participate in a micro life and health insurance scheme compared to those from the richest quintile (Table D. 5), it seems that the poorest households have rather limited access to micro life and health insurance policies. Furthermore, land ownership underlines this positive association for the uptake of any microinsurance type in the second specification (Table D. 5).

From the predictions of the underlying standard neoclassical model and of the model of life insurance demand developed by Lewis (1989), we expected a positive relationship between the degree of risk aversion and the participation in any type of microinsurance. We confirm this expectation, as households which perceived themselves as being more exposed to risk, are significantly more likely to participate in a micro health insurance scheme in the second specification (Table D. 5). This implies that micro health insurance seems to been seen by the households in Sri Lanka as a risk coping mechanism and not as an additional risk.

Interestingly, we confirm that the situation differs depending on whether and how the exposure of shocks, i.e. the tested three risk dummies, is associated with the participation in any type of microinsurance. It appears that the experience of a household member's death is significantly positively related with the participation in a micro health insurance scheme in the first specification and with the uptake of any other kind of insurance in the second. The experience of a severe illness is significantly negatively related to the use of any other insurance type. The same is true for the experience of any additional other severe shock for the uptake of micro life or any other form of insurance. Therefore, it seems plausible that households who have experienced a family related shock – namely a death of a household member – have a higher incentive to secure for the negative outcome of such a shock in the future, whereas after the experience of a household member's illness or any other severe shock the households may not regard insurance as an appropriate risk management tool, as they may not have the abilities and financial resources for the purchase, or their access may be restricted.

4.6 Conclusion

Deviating from existing contributions in the literature, this study aims to estimate three sequential steps of a household's microinsurance participation decision and subsequently analyse the factors affecting a household's decision to participate in a particular type of microinsurance. Resulting from this, we find that the residuals of two of the estimated correlation coefficients are significantly negatively correlated. Our estimations show evidence that the participation, either in life and any other form of insurance, or in health and any other form of insurance, are conflicting alternatives for the households.

Additionally, the results of our study, using the household survey data of 330 households in Sri Lanka, reveal several patterns which contribute to the literature on the determinants of participation in different types of microinsurance. First, female-headship of a household is positively associated with enrolment in an MFI and the use of micro health insurance in Sri Lanka. The same is true for married household heads. Microinsurance providers, especially in the case of micro health insurance, should take into consideration the higher propensity of female-headed households to participate in such schemes.

Second, household size is negatively linked with membership in an MFI, but positively associated with the usage of micro life insurance – presumably due to an intended bequest motive – and any other form of microinsurance in Sri Lanka. Third, there appears to be no life-cycle effect at all, but a u-shaped pattern may be noted. Fourth, we confirm that remittances may function as an additional financial resource for a household's MFI membership and microinsurance participation.

Fifth, we find that the poor are less likely to enter any of the MFIs in the study and also to use microinsurance. In short, the poor are less likely to participate in a micro life and micro health insurance scheme in Sri Lanka. It is important to note that the microinsurance products we study here do not reach the most vulnerable households, households which are most in need of microinsurance. Therefore, it would be necessary to establish two strong pillars for a higher uptake of microinsurance products: (1) the extension of the outreach through governmental or donor support of capacity building in existing MFIs and (2) more inclusive microinsurance products, i.e. better suitability to and a higher financial inclusion of the poor, which also has to be supported by practitioners, policy makers and other stakeholders. From a household perspective, it is crucial to obtain efficient risk management measures for asset building, wealth creation and hence social protection. As microinsurance is also motivated by the lack of sufficient social security measures, especially social health insurance systems, another option would be the provision of affordable public social security measures to protect the poor from consequences related to family associated shocks. If the government seems unable to meet the social security needs of the very poor, it would be necessary to invent specific products for these target groups, adapt existing microinsurance schemes and address the poor by adequate marketing and distribution channels.

Sixth, there is evidence that the educational level of the household head is a strong determinant of a household's MFI enrolment and microinsurance participation in Sri Lanka. Therefore, the implementation and promotion of insurance education measures by the providing MFIs would be essential in order to improve a household's understanding of and knowledge about insurance, while reducing mistrust in the providing institutions among possible target groups and existing clients in the communities. Further, it would be necessary to establish better training facilities and resources for the MFI staff members, so that they are able to distribute microinsurance products honestly and transparently. Both measures may lead, in the long run, to more financially capable individuals and households, especially in the rural communities. However, we did not collect data to study households' capabilities for microinsurance participation, so that this remains an area for further research. It would be desirable to conduct randomized experiments in this area.

Seventh, in contrast to earlier findings, there is evidence that households which perceived themselves as more exposed to risks are positively associated with the use of microinsurance in general, in particular micro health insurance. It seems plausible that the households in question do not see microinsurance as an additional risk. This may be traced back to the long presence of the providing MFIs in Sri Lanka, so that reliable institutions seem to play a key role by implementing new product concepts such as microinsurance.

Finally, we stated in the beginning that family related shocks are key future risks faced by households, which are mainly comprised of idiosyncratic, low loss and single-event types of risk. Interestingly, there is evidence in our estimates that the household's experience of a family related shock is positively related to the use of any of the existing microinsurance programmes under examination. This implies that existing programmes have the potential to function as effective ex ante risk management strategies which can protect households from the potentially catastrophic expenditures associated with family related shocks. Nevertheless, there is still a strong need to build up an insurance culture of the poor by extending their access to microinsurance through the increased adaptation of the product features to the needs of the target groups, i.e. the most vulnerable population groups in the regions under study, building on the experiences from informal measures and existing products in Sri Lanka.

Appendix A

Table A. 1: Definition of Explanatory Variables

Variable	Description
Willingness to take risks	Dummy variable, 1 if household ranks itself as risk loving, i.e. answers 4 or 5 on a scale from 0 (unwilling to take risks) to 5 (willing to take risks).
Illness	Dummy variable, 1 if household head was ill or injured in previous year, 0 otherwise.
Vaccination	Dummy variable, 1 if household head has received any vaccination, 0 otherwise.
Risk assessment	Household's assessment of own risk situation (subjective exposure to health shocks, road or work accidents, and economic shocks compared with neighbours), index created by factor analysis; higher index implies higher risk exposure.
Death experience	Dummy variable, 1 if household experienced the death of a household member in the previous five years and this shock had serious consequences; i.e., if household needed more than one month to recover, 0 otherwise.
Illness experience	Dummy variable, 1 if household experienced the illness of a household member in the previous five years and this shock had serious consequences; i.e., if household needed more than one month to recover, 0 otherwise.
Other shock experience	Dummy variable, 1 if household experienced a shock other than death or illness of a household member in the previous five years and this shock had serious consequences; i.e., if household needed more than one month to recover, 0 otherwise.
Age	Age of the household head.
Age squared	Age of the household head squared.
Share of dependents	Share of dependents in the total number of household members.
Married	Dummy variable, 1 if household head is married, 0 otherwise.
Benin	Dummy variable, 1 if household resides in Benin, 0 otherwise.
Female head	Dummy variable, 1 if household is headed by a female, 0 otherwise.
Schooling	Number of schooling years of the household head.
Employee/ employer	Dummy variable, 1 if household head is wage-employed or an employer herself, 0 otherwise.
Assets	Assets (bicycle, another house, refrigerator, electric iron, mobile phone, radio, TV, stove, use of electricity as main lighting source, building materials of higher quality, and toilet facilities of higher quality) owned by the household five years ago, index created by factor analysis.

Land (ln)	Log of size (in acres) of land used by the household, per adult equivalent.
Remittances	Dummy variable, 1 if household receives any remittances from former household members who have migrated, 0 otherwise.

Source: Authors' illustration.

Table A. 2: Subjective Probability of Risk Index by Factor Analysis

Variables	Description	Factor Loadings	Uniqueness
Exposure to health shocks	Dummy variable, 1 if household feels much more or a bit more exposed to health shocks in the village (risk averse to health shocks), 0 if households feels about the same, a bit less or much less exposed to respective shocks.	0.8375	0.2987
Exposure to road or working accidents	Dummy variable, 1 if household feels much more or a bit more exposed to road or working accidents shocks in the village (risk averse to road or working accidents shocks), 0 if households feels about the same, a bit less or much less exposed to respective shocks.	0.3101	0.9038
Exposure to economic shocks	Dummy variable, 1 if household feels much more or a bit more exposed to economic shocks in the village (risk averse to economic shocks), 0 if households feels about the same, a bit less or much less exposed to respective shocks.	0.7225	0.4780

Source: Authors' calculation

Note: Results of the factor analysis are estimated by the principal component factor method. Sample size is N = 350 observations.

Table A. 3: Binary Probits on the Use of Financial Services

Independent variables	(1) Microinsurance			(2) Formal savings			(3) Informal savings			(4) Formal credit			(5) Informal credit		
	Coeff.	t-stat.	MEs	Coeff.	t-stat.	MEs	Coeff.	t-stat.	MEs	Coeff.	t-stat.	MEs	Coeff.	t-stat.	MEs
Willingness to take risks	0.16	1.13	0.008	0.09	0.47	0.030	0.01	0.03	0.002	0.09	0.45	0.016	0.18	1.01	0.066
Illness	0.24	1.57	0.012	0.05	0.24	0.016	0.12	0.66	0.046	-0.23	-1.09	-0.041	0.34	1.85*	0.121
Vaccination	-0.29	-1.93*	-0.015	0.46	2.54**	0.157	-0.18	-1.01	-0.070	0.56	2.75***	0.099	-0.15	-0.85	-0.055
Risk assessment	-0.09	-1.15	-0.004	-0.01	-0.14	-0.004	-0.23	-2.69***	-0.093	0.01	0.07	0.001	0.18	2.03**	0.065
Death experience	0.11	0.68	0.005	0.28	1.39	0.098	0.36	1.99**	0.143	0.22	0.98	0.039	0.68	3.59***	0.247
Illness experience	-0.02	-0.15	-0.001	0.21	1.05	0.074	0.57	3.04***	0.225	0.46	2.07**	0.090	0.51	2.67***	0.187
Other shock experience	0.08	0.34	0.004	0.29	1.02	0.107	0.04	0.14	0.015	0.93	3.01***	0.239	0.41	1.58	0.157
Age	0.15	3.74***	0.007	0.03	1.03	0.011	-0.07	-2.45**	-0.028	0.09	2.69***	0.016	0.08	2.31**	0.027
Age squared	-0.00	-3.71***	-0.000	-0.00	-0.67	-0.000	0.00	1.98**	0.000	-0.00	-2.42**	-0.000	-0.00	-2.82***	-0.000
Share of dependents	0.04	0.13	0.002	-0.22	-0.68	-0.076	0.82	2.68***	0.326	-0.50	-1.50	-0.090	0.22	0.71	0.080
Married	-0.05	-0.25	-0.002	0.26	1.18	0.090	-0.37	-1.79*	-0.146	0.59	2.69***	0.097	0.24	1.06	0.084
Benin	0.72	4.33***	0.056	0.13	0.59	0.045	0.30	1.54	0.119	-0.18	-0.78	-0.030	-0.09	-0.49	-0.035
Female head	0.07	0.35	0.003	-0.54	-2.34**	-0.183	-0.48	-2.24**	-0.188	-0.09	-0.45	-0.017	-0.04	-0.18	-0.014
Schooling	0.04	2.61***	0.002	0.06	2.97***	0.019	-0.04	-2.00**	-0.014	0.04	1.88*	0.007	-0.04	-1.82*	-0.013
Employee/ employer	0.04	0.17	0.002	0.99	3.68***	0.373	-0.28	-1.13	-0.111	0.50	2.08**	0.111	0.27	1.09	0.101
Assets	0.36	4.67***	0.017	0.29	3.00***	0.104	0.39	3.90***	0.155	0.20	2.07**	0.036	0.04	0.35	0.013
Land (ln)	-0.16	-1.07	-0.008	0.02	0.11	0.006	-0.17	-1.07	-0.066	0.19	1.09	0.033	0.08	0.49	0.027
Remittances	-0.16	-0.89	-0.007	0.49	2.47**	0.177	-0.01	-0.04	-0.003	0.11	0.52	0.021	0.22	1.08	0.080

Source: Authors' calculation.

Note: The model also includes a constant. Sample size is N = 350 observations. Households in the sample are weighted according to their sampling probabilities. The asterisks indicate level of significance: *** significant at 1 percent, ** significant at 5 percent, * significant at 10 percent.

Table A. 4: Multivariate Probit Results for Different Categories of Insurance

Independent variables	(1) Anidaso only (Mean = 0.045)			(2) NHIS only (Mean = 0.262)			(3) All Insurance (Anidaso, NHIS, Other) (Mean = 0.306)		
	Coeff.	**t-stat.**	**APE**	**Coeff.**	**t-stat.**	**APE**	**Coeff.**	**t-stat.**	**APE**
Willingness to take risks	0.201	9.164***	0.023	-0.258	-1.50	-0.101	-0.127	-0.76	-0.045
Illness	0.255	1.534	0.029	0.579	13.95***	0.223	0.627	11.48***	0.228
Vaccination	-0.233	-9.151***	-0.032	0.064	0.55	0.024	-0.076	-0.92	-0.028
Risk assessment	-0.094	-6.193***	-0.014	-0.111	-2.96***	-0.040	-0.1333	-3.99***	-0.052
Death experience	0.043	0.780	0.006	0.328	3.10***	0.125	0.238	2.99***	0.069
Illness experience	0.019	0.172	0.003	0.075	0.81	0.031	0.204	3.40***	0.058
Other shock experience	-0.034	-0.549	-0.005	0.202	1.51	0.077	0.191	2.29**	0.046
Age	0.169	6.090***	0.013	-0.032	-1.49	-0.010	-0.20	-0.70	-0.007
Age squared	-0.002	-5.468***	-0.000	0.001	2.54**	0.000	0.000	1.48	0.000
Share of dependents	0.053	0.495	0.008	0.163	5.72***	0.057	0.070	0.72	0.026
Married	-0.096	-0.574	-0.011	0.010	0.20	0.004	0.090	2.62***	0.032
Benin	0.688	3.351***	0.122	0.588	7.33***	0.191	0.768	9.00***	0.129
Female head	-0.030	-0.190	-0.004	-0.113	-0.71	-0.043	0.112	1.43	0.040
Schooling	0.039	2.54**	0.004	0.039	3.65***	0.012	0.053	5.26***	0.019
Employee/ employer	0.033	0.278	0.005	0.253	2.76***	0.094	0.461	10.66***	0.184
Assets	0.374	2.930***	0.049	0.308	3.20***	0.110	0.407	5.57***	0.160
Land (ln)	-0.083	-1.195	-0.013	-0.197	-5.31***	-0.072	-0.062	-3.94***	-0.026
Remittances	-0.189	-2.021**	-0.026	0.325	5.37***	0.126	0.203	2.76***	0.075

Source: Authors' calculation

Note: Results of the multivariate probit model are estimated by simulated maximum likelihood with 50 pseudorandom draws. t-statistics refer to the estimated coefficients and are based on robust standard errors. Average partial effects (APEs) are calculated with respect to the marginal probability of each type of financial service. The model also includes a constant. Sample size is N = 350 observations. Households in the sample are weighted according to their sampling probabilities. Wald test of the model (1): $X^2 = 17.21$; $p = 0.0002$; Wald test of the model (2): $X^2 = 28.89$; $p = 0.0000$; Wald test of the model (3): $X^2 = 4.41$; $p = 0.1105$. The asterisks indicate level of significance: *** significant at 1 percent, ** significant at 5 percent, * significant at 10 percent.

Appendix B

Table B. 1: Definition of Explanatory Variables

Variable	Description
Household's self-perception of risk	Household's assessment of own risk situation (subjective exposure to health shocks, weather and environmental related shocks, and economic shocks compared with neighbours, own rating of willingness to take risks), index created by factor analysis.
Drought	Dummy variable, 1 if household experienced a drought in the last five years and this shock had serious consequences, i.e. household needed more than one month to recover, 0 otherwise.
Animal threat	Dummy variable, 1 if household experienced an animal threat in the last five years and this shock had serious consequences, i.e. household needed more than one month to recover, 0 otherwise.
Crop failure	Dummy variable, 1 if household experienced a crop failure in the last five years and this shock had serious consequences, i.e. household needed more than one month to recover, 0 otherwise.
Death experience	Dummy variable, 1 if household experienced the death of a household member in the last five years and this shock had serious consequences, i.e. household needed more than one month to recover, 0 otherwise.
Illness experience	Dummy variable, 1 if household experienced the illness of a household member in the last five years and this shock had serious consequences, i.e. household needed more than one month to recover, 0 otherwise.
Input	Dummy variable, 1 if household experienced an increase in input prices in the last five years and this shock had serious consequences, i.e. household needed more than one month to recover, 0 otherwise.
No ability to sell agricultural products	Dummy variable, 1 if household experienced an inability to sell agricultural products in the last five years and this shock had serious consequences, i.e. household needed more than one month to recover, 0 otherwise.
Other shock experience	Dummy variable, 1 if household experienced a severe shock other than the previous described shock in the last five years and this shock had serious consequences, i.e. household needed more than one month to recover, 0 otherwise.
Household size	Household size.
Age	Age of the household head.
Age squared	Age of the household head squared.
No or only primary education	Dummy variable, 1 if household has no or only primary education, 0 otherwise.
Secondary education	Dummy variable, 1 if household has secondary education, 0 otherwise.
Self-employed	Dummy variable, 1 if household head is self-employed or a contractual

	worker in either agriculture or non-agricultural activities, 0 otherwise.
Not employed	Dummy variable, 1 if household head is not employed due to young or old age, disability, or similar reasons, 0 otherwise.
Distance to road	Distance to nearest access road in metres.
Remittances	Dummy variable, 1 if household receives remittances from former household members who have migrated, 0 otherwise.
Land ownership	Dummy variable, if the household owns any land, 0 otherwise.
Assets	Assets index.
Quintiles 1 - 5	Five asset index quintiles labelled as Quintile 1 to 5, Quintile 1 is the poorest quintile and Quintile 5 is the quintile of households with the highest asset endowment. Dummy variables, 1 if household belongs to the asset index quintile, 0 otherwise (Quintile 5 functions as the reference category).

Source: Authors' illustration.

Table B. 2: Subjective Probability of Risk Index by Factor Analysis

Variables	Description	Factor Loadings	Uniqueness
Exposure to health shocks	Dummy variable, 1 if household feels much more or a bit more exposed to health shocks in the village (risk averse to health shocks), 0 if household feels about the same, a bit less or much less exposed to respective shocks.	0.7796	0.3922
Exposure to weather and environment related shocks	Dummy variable, 1 if household feels much more or a bit more exposed to weather and environmental related shocks in the village (risk averse to weather and environmental related shocks shocks), 0 if household feels about the same, a bit less or much less exposed to respective shocks.	0.5508	0.6966
Exposure to economic shocks	Dummy variable, 1 if household feels much more or a bit more exposed to economic shocks in the village (risk averse to economic shocks), 0 if household feels about the same, a bit less or much less exposed to respective shocks.	0.6889	0.5254
Household's own rating of willingness to take risks	Dummy variable, 1 if a household head rates himself as risk averse, i.e. unwilling to take risks (values 0 to 2), 0 if a household head rates himself as willing to take risks (values 3-5). (Question: Are you rather willing or unwilling to take risks?, Please rank on a scale where the value 0 means "unwilling to take risks" and the value 5 means "willing to take risks".	0.2020	0.9592

Source: Authors' calculation

Note: Results of the factor analysis are estimated by the principal component factor method. Sample size is N = 330 observations.

Table B. 3: Correlation Matrix of Explanatory Variables

Variables	Household's self-perception of risk	Drought	Animal threat	Crop failure	Death	Illness	Input	Agricultural products	Other shock	Female head
Household's self-perception of risk	1.00									
Drought	-0.03	1.00								
Animal threat	0.05	0.47	1.00							
Crop failure	0.06	0.14	0.17	1.00						
Death	0.02	-0.03	-0.04	0.05	1.00					
Illness	0.09	-0.02	-0.03	0.08	-0.0	1.00				
Input	-0.01	0.22	0.23	0.19	-0.04	-0.01	1.00			
Agricultural products	-0.03	0.49	0.28	0.21	-0.04	0.01	0.33	1.00		
Other shock	0.01	-0.12	-0.09	-0.09	-0.09	-0.13	-0.15	-0.09	1.00	
Female head	-0.01	0.06	0.10	0.02	0.18	-0.09	0.06	-0.01	0.04	1.00
Household size	0.04	-0.04	-0.05	0.11	0.01	0.13	0.04	0.06	0.10	-0.25
Age	0.15	-0.02	0.03	0.00	0.02	0.10	0.03	-0.01	-0.08	0.17
Age squared	0.17	-0.02	0.02	0.02	0.03	0.11	0.03	-0.02	-0.07	0.16
No or only primary	0.17	0.01	0.02	0.07	0.07	0.07	-0.01	0.06	0.02	0.13
Secondary	-0.08	0.00	-0.00	0.02	-0.07	0.07	0.02	0.03	-0.00	-0.02
Self-employed	-0.03	0.19	0.11	0.05	0.02	0.02	0.04	0.15	0.02	-0.04
Not employed	0.09	-0.13	-0.05	-0.01	0.02	0.05	-0.01	-0.08	0.05	0.19
Distance	-0.02	-0.04	-0.09	-0.09	0.05	-0.05	-0.09	-0.01	-0.00	-0.03
Remittance	-0.06	-0.00	0.13	0.09	-0.01	0.02	0.10	-0.02	-0.03	0.22
Land	0.03	0.19	0.08	0.13	0.07	-0.03	0.16	0.16	0.06	0.03
Assets	-0.12	-0.18	-0.14	0.14	-0.03	-0.03	0.08	-0.01	-0.01	-0.11

Variables	Household size	Age	Age squared	No or only primary education	Secondary education	Self-employed	Not employed	Distance to market	Remittance	Land	Assets
Household's self-perception of risk											
Drought											
Animal threat											
Crop failure											
Death											
Illness											
Input											
Agricultural products											
Other shock											
Female head											
Household size	1.00										
Age	0.09	1.00									
Age squared	0.08	0.98	1.00								
No or only primary	0.15	0.36	0.37	1.00							
Secondary	0.00	-0.01	-0.03	-0.40	1.00						
Self-employed	0.05	-0.11	-0.13	0.04	0.04	1.00					
Not employed	-0.01	0.34	0.37	0.17	-0.03	-0.65	1.00				
Distance	-0.16	-0.13	-0.12	0.01	-0.08	0.17	-0.10	1.00			
Remittance	-0.03	0.18	0.19	0.17	-0.08	-0.03	0.11	-0.04	1.00		
Land	0.08	0.06	0.06	0.04	-0.15	-0.05	0.028	-0.30	0.02	1.00	
Assets	0.11	-0.03	-0.03	-0.19	-0.11	-0.11	-0.03	-0.14	0.02	0.07	1.00
Source:	Authors' calculation										

Appendix C

Table C. 1: Definition of Explanatory Variables

Variable	Description
Female head	Dummy variable, 1 if household is headed by a female, 0 otherwise.
Dependents	Number of all dependents, i.e. old and young, in the household.
Children	Number of children in the household.
Old dependents	Number of old dependents, i.e. retired or economically inactive persons due to age, in the household.
Married	Dummy variable, 1 if household head is married, 0 otherwise.
Age	Age of the household head.
Age squared	Age of the household head squared.
No or only primary education	Dummy variable, 1 if household has no or only primary education, 0 otherwise.
Secondary education	Dummy variable, 1 if household has secondary education, 0 otherwise.
Head is self-employed	Dummy variable, 1 if household head is self-employed or a contractual worker in either agriculture or non-agricultural activities, 0 otherwise.
Head is unemployed	Dummy variable, 1 if household head is not employed due to youth or old age, disability, or similar reasons, 0 otherwise.
Assets	Assets (motorcycle, bicycle, jewellery, refrigerator, sewing machine, electric iron, water heater, fan, TV, DVD, radio, fixed phone, mobile phone, main source of drinking, toilet facility, main source of lighting) owned by the household and not purchased by a loan, index created by factor analysis.
Quintiles 1 - 5	Five asset index quintiles labeled as Quintile 1 to 5, Quintile 1 is the poorest quintile and Quintile 5 is the quintile of households with the highest asset endowment. Dummy variables, 1 if household belong to the asset index quintile, 0 otherwise (Quintile 5 functions as reference category).
Land ownership	Dummy variable, if the household owns any land, 0 otherwise.
Household's self-perception of risk	Household's self-perception of its own risk exposure (subjective exposure to health shocks, weather and environmental related shocks, and economic shocks compared with neighbors, plus own rating of willingness to take risks), index created by factor analysis.
Experienced illness of a household member	Dummy variable, 1 if household experienced the illness of a household member in the last five years and this shock had serious consequences, i.e. household needed more than one month to recover, 0 otherwise
Experienced	Dummy variable, 1 if household experienced the death of a household

death of a household member	member in the last five years and this shock had serious consequences, i.e. household needed more than one month to recover, 0 otherwise.
Experienced other severe (catastrophic) event	Dummy variable, 1 if household experienced a severe shock other than the previous described shock in the last five years and this shock had serious consequences, i.e. household needed more than one month to recover, 0 otherwise.
Distance to road	Distance to nearest access road in metres.
Buddhist	Dummy variable, 1 if household head is Buddhist, and 0 otherwise (reference category for the two religious dummies is "Head is Christian").
Hindu	Dummy variable, 1 if household head is Hindu, and 0 otherwise (reference category for the two religious dummies is "Head is Christian").
Regions	Dummy variables, 1 if household resides in the region, and 0 otherwise. Nine dummy variables (Western, Southern, North Western, North, Central, Sabara, North Central, Uva and Western region) are used in the analysis. Central region functions as the reference category.

Source: Authors' illustration.

Table C. 2: Summary Statistics: Insurance Buyers vs. Non-Buyers

Variable	Full Sample		Insurance Buyers		Insurance Non-Buyers	
	Mean	Std. error	Mean	Std. error	Mean	Std. error
Female head	0.169	0.021	0.163	0.024	0.189	0.041
Dependents	2.633	0.074	2.663	0.089	2.556	0.133
Children	1.015	0.058	1.058	0.068	0.900	0.108
Old dependents	1.618	0.065	1.604	0.0796	1.656	0.111
Married	0.861	0.019	0.871	0.021	0.833	0.039
Age	47.88	0.644	47.41	0.744	49.12	1.280
Age squared	2428.7	64.5	2379.9	73.2	2558.8	132.9
No or only primary education	0.191	0.021	0.171	0.024	0.244	0.046
Secondary education	0.409	0.027	0.40	0.032	0.433	0.053
Head is self-employed	0.594	0.027	0.579	0.032	0.633	0.051
Head is unemployed	0.221	0.023	0.221	0.027	0.222	0.044
Asset index	-1.9e-09	0.055	0.126	0.064	-0.337	0.102
Quintile 1	0.2	0.022	0.167	0.024	0.289	0.048
Quintile 2	0.2	0.022	0.179	0.025	0.256	0.046
Quintile 3	0.2	0.022	0.2	0.026	0.2	0.042
Quintile 4	0.2	0.022	0.221	0.027	0.144	0.037
Land ownership	0.773	0.023	0.825	0.025	0.633	0.051
Household's self-perception of risk	9.9e-09	0.168	0.009	0.067	-0.025	0.093
Experienced death of a household member	0.073	0.014	0.071	0.017	0.078	0.028
Experienced severe illness of a household member	0.142	0.019	0.158	0.024	0.1	0.031
Experienced other severe (catastrophic) event	0.336	0.026	0.333	0.030	0.344	0.050
Distance to road	299.52	36.85	281.86	40.86	346.63	80.08
Head is Buddhist	0.903	0.016	0.908	0.019	0.889	0.033
Head is Hindu	0.054	0.013	0.038	0.012	0.100	0.031
Observations	330		240		90	

Source: Authors' calculation.

Table C. 3: Estimates of Probit Regression Model of Insurance Uptake

Variable	Insurance Participation All Age Groups		Insurance Participation Under 65 Years only	
	MEs	**z-stat.**	**MEs**	**z-stat.**
Female head	-0.0013	-0.77	-0.0014	-0.63
Children	0.0035	3.40***	0.0027	2.59***
Old dependents	0.0006	0.82	0.0008	0.91
Married	-0.0039	-0.41	-0.0032	-0.31
Age	-0.0018	-2.51***	-0.0009	-1.02
Age squared	0.00001	2.41***	7.25e-06	0.69
No or only primary education	0.2596	1.90*	0.3441	1.96**
Secondary education	0.0108	1.97**	0.0086	1.80*
Head is self-employed	0.0029	1.33	0.0036	1.49
Head is unemployed	-0.00003	-0.01	0.0028	0.57
Asset index	0.0087	3.74***	0.0094	3.55***
Land ownership	0.0019	1.61	0.0016	1.17
Household's self-perception of risk	0.0011	1.57	0.0005	0.50
Experienced death of a household member	0.0623	0.83	0.1211	0.93
Experienced severe illness of a household member	0.00006	0.03	0.0017	0.43
Experienced other severe (catastrophic) event	-0.0073	-1.71*	-0.0055	-1.40
Market access: distance to road	-1.23e-06	-0.65	-8.31e-07	-0.40
Head is Buddhist	-0.8778	-5.55***	-0.8999	-7.23***
Head is Hindu	-0.0015	-2.87***	-0.0016	-2.68***
Regional dummies	Yes	-	Yes	-
Observations	330		301	

Source: Authors' Calculation.

Note: For the probit model, coefficients are normalized to display marginal effects (MEs). Regression also includes regional dummy variables (outcome omitted). * significant at 10%, ** significant at 5%, *** significant at 1%.

Appendix D

Table D. 1: Definition of Explanatory Variables for Sri Lanka

Variable	Description
Female head	Dummy variable, 1 if household is headed by a female, 0 otherwise.
Household size	Household size.
Married head	Dummy variable, 1 if household head is married, 0 otherwise.
Ratio of ill household members	Ratio of ill household members in the previous 12 months to the total number of household members.
Age	Age of the household head.
Age squared	Age of the household head squared.
No or only primary education	Dummy variable, 1 if household has no or only primary education, 0 otherwise.
Secondary education	Dummy variable, 1 if household has secondary education, 0 otherwise.
Head is self-employed	Dummy variable, 1 if household head is self-employed or a contractual worker in either agriculture or non-agricultural activities, 0 otherwise.
Head is unemployed	Dummy variable, 1 if household head is not employed due to young or old age, disability, or similar reasons, 0 otherwise.
Assets	Assets (motorcycle, bicycle, jewellery, refrigerator, sewing machine, electric iron, water heater, fan, TV, DVD, radio, fixed phone, mobile phone, main source of drinking, toilet facility, main source of lighting) owned by the household and was not purchased by a loan, index created by factor analysis.
Quintile 1-5	Five asset index quintiles labeled as Quintile 1 to 5, Quintile 1 is the poorest quintile and Quintile 5 is the quintile of households with the highest asset endowment. Dummy variables, 1 if household belong to the asset index quintile, 0 otherwise (Quintile 5 functions as reference category).
Land ownership	Dummy variable, if the household owns any land, 0 otherwise.
Remittance	Dummy variable, 1 if household receives remittances from former household members who have migrated, 0 otherwise.
Household's self-perception of risk	Household's assessment of own risk situation (subjective exposure to health shocks, weather and environment related shocks, and economic shocks compared with neighbours, own rating of willingness to take risks), index created by factor analysis.
Experienced death a of household member	Dummy variable, 1 if household experienced the death of a household member in the last five years and this shock had serious consequences, i.e. household needed more than one month to recover, 0 otherwise.
Experienced illness of a household mem-	Dummy variable, 1 if household experienced the illness of a household member in the last five years and this shock had serious consequences, i.e. household needed more than one month to recover, 0 otherwise.

ber	
Experienced other severe shock	Dummy variable, 1 if household experienced a severe shock other than the previous described shock in the last five years and this shock had serious consequences, i.e. household needed more than one month to recover, 0 otherwise.
Loca-tional/Regional dummies	Dummy variables, 1 if household resides in the region, and 0 otherwise. Nine dummy variables (Western, Southern, North Western, North, Cen-tral, Sabara, North Central, Uva and Western region) are used in the analysis. The Central region functions a reference category.

Source: Authors' illustration.

Table D. 2: Summary Statistics: Insurance Buyers vs. Non-Buyers

Variable	**Full Sample**		**Insurance Buyers**		**Insurance Non-Buyers**	
	Mean	Std. error	Mean	Std. error	Mean	Std. error
Female head	0.169	0.021	0.163	0.024	0.189	0.041
Household size	4.094	0.078	4.204	0.091	3.800	0.148
Married head	0.861	0.019	0.871	0.021	0.833	0.039
Ratio of ill household members	0.393	0.023	0.409	0.027	0.349	0.042
Age	47.88	0.644	47.41	0.744	49.12	1.280
Age squared	2428.7	64.5	2379.9	73.2	2558.8	132.9
Education of household head (base: tertiary education)						
No or only primary education	0.191	0.021	0.171	0.024	0.244	0.046
Secondary education	0.409	0.027	0.40	0.032	0.433	0.053
Occupation of household head (base: formal employee/employer)						
Head is self-employed	0.594	0.027	0.579	0.032	0.633	0.051
Head is unemployed	0.221	0.023	0.221	0.027	0.222	0.044
Asset index	-1.9e-09	0.055	0.126	0.064	-0.337	0.102
Quintile 1	0.2	0.022	0.167	0.024	0.289	0.048
Quintile 2	0.2	0.022	0.179	0.025	0.256	0.046
Quintile 3	0.2	0.022	0.2	0.026	0.2	0.042
Quintile 4	0.2	0.022	0.221	0.027	0.144	0.037
Land ownership	0.773	0.023	0.825	0.025	0.633	0.051
Remittance	0.051	0.012	0.054	0.015	0.044	0.022
Household's self-perception of risk	9.9e-09	0.168	0.009	0.067	-0.025	0.093
Household's risk experience (base: no risk experience)						
Experienced death of a household member	0.073	0.014	0.071	0.017	0.078	0.028
Experienced severe illness of a household member	0.142	0.019	0.158	0.024	0.1	0.031
Experienced other severe shock	0.336	0.026	0.333	0.030	0.344	0.050
Observations	330		240		90	

Source: Authors' calculation.

Table D. 3: Summary Statistics: Life, Health and other Insurance Buyers vs. Non-Buyers

Variable	**Full Sample**		**Life Insurance Buyers**		**Health Insurance Buyers**		**Other Insurance Buyers**	
	Mean	Std. error	Mean	Std. error	Mean	Std. error	Mean	Std. error
Female head	0.169	0.021	0.148	0.029	0.138	0.065	0.177	0.043
Household size	4.094	0.078	4.296	0.126	4.345	0.245	4.013	0.142
Married head	0.861	0.019	0.880	0.027	0.931	0.048	0.848	0.041
Ratio of ill household members	0.393	0.023	0.397	0.034	0.413	0.069	0.425	0.050
Age	47.88	0.644	48.23	0.973	50.21	2.019	45.63	1.267
Age squared	2428.7	64.5	2,459.9	96.77	2634.9	207.84	2207.6	121.37
Education of household head (base: tertiary education)								
No or only primary education	0.191	0.021	0.183	0.033	0.241	0.081	0.127	0.038
Secondary education	0.409	0.027	0.408	0.041	0.517	0.094	0.367	0.054
Occupation of household head (base: formal employee/employer)								
Head is self-employed	0.594	0.027	0.648	0.040	0.517	0.094	0.481	0.057
Head is unemployed	0.221	0.023	0.218	0.035	0.207	0.077	0.228	0.047
Asset index	-1.9e-09	0.055	0.180	0.083	0.112	0.196	0.121	0.106
Quintile 1	0.2	0.022	0.148	0.029	0.241	0.081	0.152	0.041
Quintile 2	0.2	0.022	0.176	0.032	0.069	0.048	0.203	0.046
Quintile 3	0.2	0.022	0.211	0.034	0.276	0.084	0.164	0.042
Quintile 4	0.2	0.022	0.190	0.033	0.138	0.065	0.304	0.052
Land ownership	0.773	0.023	0.845	0.030	0.793	0.077	0.797	0.046
Remittance	0.051	0.012	0.056	0.019	0.069	0.048	0.051	0.025
Household's self-perception of risk	9.9e-09	0.168	-0.054	0.073	0.086	0.212	0.062	0.136
Household's risk experience (base: no risk experience)								
Experienced death of a household member	0.073	0.014	0.070	0.012	0.034	0.034	0.076	0.029
Experienced severe illness of a household member	0.142	0.019	0.190	0.033	0.345	0.089	0.076	0.029
Experienced other severe shock	0.336	0.026	0.373	0.041	0.414	0.093	0.203	0.046
Observations	330		142		29		79	

Source: Authors' calculation.

Table D. 4: Binary Probits on Insurance Participation for Sri Lanka

Variable	Specification (I)	Specification (II)
Female head	0.001	-0.001
Household size	0.003***	0.003***
Age	-0.002***	-0.002***
Age squared	0.00002**	0.00002**
Education of household head (base: tertiary education)		
No or only primary education	0.205*	0.089
Secondary education	0.009*	0.008
Occupation of household head (base: formal employee/employer)		
Head is self-employed	0.003	0.00006
Head is unemployed	0.0006	-0.002
Asset index	0.009***	-
Asset quintiles (base: the richest 20%)		
Quintile 1	-	-0.249***
Quintile 2	-	-0.069***
Quintile 3	-	-0.024***
Quintile 4	-	0.001
Land ownership	0.002	0.006***
Remittance	0.055	0.059
Household's self-perception of risk	0.001**	0.002*
Household's risk experience (base: no risk experience)		
Experienced death of a household member	0.204	0.036
Experienced severe illness of a household member	-0.001	-0.002**
Experienced other severe shock	-0.012*	-0.022**
Locational/regional dummies	Yes	Yes
Observations	330	330

Source: Authors' calculation.

Note: Probit model. Coefficients are normalized to display marginal effects (MEs). The asterisks indicate level of significance (Robust z-statistics): *** significant at 1 percent, ** significant at 5 percent, * significant at 10 percent.

Table D. 5: Multivariate Probit Results on the Type of Insurance for Sri Lanka (II)

Variable	Life Insurance			Health Insurance			Other Insurance		
	Coeff.	APEs	z-stat.	Coeff.	APEs	z-stat.	Coeff.	APEs	z-stat.
Female head	-0.457	-0.071	-0.69	1.392	0.0006	2.45***	-0.510	-0.023	-0.83
Household size	0.141	0.029	1.18	0.191	6.90e-06	1.34	0.338	0.029	2.31**
Married head	-0.313	-0.068	-0.59	0.864	8.55e-06	1.00	-1.354	-0.206	-2.63***
Ratio of ill household members	0.246	0.054	0.27	0.151	4.94e-06	0.16	-0.040	-0.002	-0.09
Age	-0.165	-0.028	-2.89***	-0.211	-3.16e-06	-2.24**	-0.119	-0.007	-1.27
Age squared	0.002	0.0003	3.01***	0.002	5.15e-08	2.80***	0.0008	0.0000 5	0.85
No or only primary education	1.588	0.462	4.11***	2.749	0.014	3.16***	-0.316	-0.016	-0.51
Secondary education	0.754	0.156	4.36***	1.801	0.0004	2.06**	0.056	0.003	0.24
Head is self-employed	0.575	0.103	1.56	-1.099	-0.00008	-2.87***	-0.332	-0.022	-1.05
Head is unemployed	0.243	0.050	0.75	-1.945	-0.00003	-3.41***	-0.421	-0.021	-1.64*
Quintile 1	-3.019	-0.269	-6.99***	-3.497	-0.0001	-4.39***	-0.654	-0.029	-0.95
Quintile 2	-2.689	-0.247	-5.92***	-3.982	-0.0002	-3.62***	-0.004	-0.0003	-0.01
Quintile 3	-2.229	-0.218	-6.48***	-1.922	-0.00003	-7.38***	-0.409	-0.020	-0.62
Quintile 4	-0.168	-0.029	-0.89	-0.473	-6.91e-06	-2.67***	1.252	0.162	2.24**
Land ownership	0.771	0.133	2.13**	-0.659	-0.00004	-0.64	0.395	0.020	2.04**
Remittance	0.362	0.083	0.50	-1.329	-6.85e-06	-1.24	2.098	0.504	1.68*
Household's self-perception of risk	0.014	0.003	0.08	0.333	0.00002	1.78*	0.040	0.003	0.33
Experienced death of a household member	0.283	0.062	0.46	-0.295	-4.17e-06	-0.55	0.817	0.097	1.96**
Experienced severe illness of a household member	0.152	0.031	0.47	0.880	0.0001	1.24	-1.093	-0.036	-1.45
Experienced other severe shock	-0.913	-0.147	-3.23***	-0.687	-0.00001	-1.49	-0.887	-0.046	-2.18**
Regional dummies	Yes	-	-	Yes	-	-	Yes	-	-
Est. correlation coeff.	ρ_{21} = 0.166	1.23		ρ_{31} = -0.712		-7.54***	ρ_{32} = -0.577	-3.91***	

Source: Authors' calculation.

Note: Results of the trivariate probit model are estimated by SML with 20 pseudorandom draws. The t-statistics refer to the estimated coefficients and are based on robust standard errors. Average partial effects (APEs) are calculated with respect to the marginal probability of each type of insurance. The model also includes a constant. Sample size is N = 240 observations. The asterisks indicate level of significance: *** significant at 1 percent, ** significant at 5 percent, * significant at 10 percent.

Bibliography

Abbring, Jaap H., Pierre-André Chiappori, James J. Heckman and Jean Pinquet (2003): Adverse Selection and Moral Hazard in Insurance: Can Dynamic Data Help to Distinguish?, *Journal of the European Economic Association, Papers and Proceedings of the Seventeenth Annual Congress of the European Economic Association (Apr. - May)* 1 (2/3), pp. 512-521.

Akerlof, George A. (1970): The Market for "Lemons", Quality Uncertainty and the Market Mechanism, *Quartely Journal of Economics*, 84, pp. 488-500.

Alderman, Harold and Christina Paxson (1994): Do the Poor Insure? A Synthesis of the Literature on Risk and Consumption in Developing Countries, In: *Economics in a Changing World, Vol.4: Development, Trade, and the Environment*, edited by E. Bacha. Basingstoke: Macmillan.

Amuedo-Dorantes, Catalina and Susan Pozo (2006): Remittances as Insurance: Evidence from Mexican Immigrants, *Journal of Population Economics*, Vol. 19, pp. 227-254.

Ando, Albert and Franco Modigliani (1963): The Life-Cycle Hypothesis of Saving: Aggregate Implications and Tests, *American Economic Review*, 53 (1, part1), pp. 55-84.

Armendáriz, Beatriz and Jonathan Morduch (2005): *The Economics of Microfinance*, Cambridge, Mass. and London: The MIT Press.

Armendáriz, Beatriz and Jonathan Morduch (2010): *The Economics of Microfinance*, 2nd Edition, Cambridge, Mass. and London: The MIT Press.

Arrow, K.J. (1965): *Aspects of the Theory of Risk-Bearing*, Yrjö Johnsson Lectures, Helsinki. [printed with changes in: Arrow, K.J. (1970): Essays in Theory of Risk-bearing, Amsterdam-London].

Aryeetey, Ernest and Christopher Udry (2000): Saving in Sub-Saharan Africa, CID Working Papers 38, Harvard University: Center for International Development.

Asfaw, A. (2003): *Cost of Illness, Demand for Medical Care, and the Prospect of Community Health Insurance Schemes in the Rural Areas of Ethiopia*, Frankfurt: Peter Lang Eds.

Asian Development Bank (ADB) (2006): Technical Assistance to Sri Lanka for Microinsurance Sector Development, Supply Assessment of Microinsurance Products. Australia: Cambridge Centre for Public Policy Development.

Atieno, R. (1997): Determinants of Credit Demand by Smallholder Farmers in Kenya: An Empirical Analysis, *Tropenlandwirt*, 98(1), pp. 63-71.

Ayalew, D. (2003): Risk Sharing Networks among Households in Rural Ethiopia, CSAE Working Paper 04/2003, Centre for the Study of African Economies, Oxford, UK.

Babbel, David F. and Eisaku Ohtsuka (1989): Aspects of Optimal Multiperiod Life Insurance, *Journal of Risk and Insurance*, 56 (3), pp. 460-481.

Barsky, R.B., F. Th. Juster, M.S. Kimball and M.D. Spapiro (1997): Preference Parameters and Behavioral Heterogeneity: an Experimental Approach in the Health and Retirement Study, *Quarterly Journal of Economics*, 112, pp. 537-579.

Barslund, Mikkel and Finn Tarp (2008): Formal and Informal Rural Credit in Four Provinces of Vietnam, *Journal of Development Studies*, 44 (4), pp. 485-503.

Basu, Anupam, Rodolphe Blavy, and Murat Yulek (2004) Microfinance in Africa: Experience and Lessons from Selected African Countries, IMF Working Paper 04/174, Washington DC: International Monetary Fund (IMF).

Bartus, Tamás (2005): Estimation of Marginal Effects Using margeff, *The Stata Journal*, 5 (3), pp. 309-329.

Beck, Thorsten and Jan Webb (2002): Economic, Demographic, and Institutional Determinants of Life Insurance Consumption Across Countries, *The World Bank Economic Review*, 17, pp. 51-88.

Bernheim, B. Douglas, Andrei Shleifer and Lawrence H. Summers (1985): The Strategic Bequest Motive, *Journal of Political Economy*, 93, pp. 1045-76.

Bernheim, B. Douglas (1991): How Strong Are Bequest Motives? Evidence Based on Estimates of the Demand for Life Insurance and Annuities, *Journal of Political Economy*, 99 (5), pp. 899-927.

Bernheim, B. Douglas, Lorenzo Forni, Jagadeesh Gokhale and Laurence J. Kotlikoff (2003): The Mismatch between Life Insurance Holdings and Financial Vulnerabilities: Evidence from the Health and Retirement Study, *American Economic Review*, 93 (1), pp. 354-365.

Besley, Timothy (1995): Savings, Credit and Insurance, In: *Handbook of Development Economics Vol. 3*, edited by J. R. Behrman, T. N. Srinivasan and H. B. Chenery. Amsterdam: Elsevier.

Bhat, Ramesh and Nishant Jain (2006): Factoring Affecting the Demand for Health Insurance in a Micro Insurance Scheme, Working Paper No. 2006-07-02, Ahmedabad: Indian Institute of Management.

Black, Kenneth and Harold D. Skipper (2000): *Life and Health Insurance*, 13th edition, Upper Saddle River: Prentice Hall.

Browne, Mark J. (1992): Evidence of Adverse Selection in the Individual Health Insurance Market, *Journal of Risk and Insurance*, 59 (1), pp. 13-33.

Browne, Mark J. and Kihong Kim (1993): An International Analysis of Life Insurance Demand, *Journal of Risk and Insurance*, 60, pp. 616-634.

Browne, Mark J. and Helen I. Doerpinghaus (1993): Information Asymmetries and Adverse Selection in the Market for Individual Medical Expense Insurance, *Journal of Risk and Insurance*, 60, pp. 300-312.

Browning, Martin, and Annamaria Lusardi (1996): Household Saving, Micro Theory and Micro Facts, *Journal of Economic Literature*, 34 (4), pp. 1797-1855.

Burnett, John J. and Bruce A. Palmer (1984): Examining Life Insurance Ownership Through Demographic and Psychographic Characteristics, *Journal of Risk and Insurance*, 51, pp. 453-467.

Cai, Hongbin, Yuyu Chen, Hanming Fang, and Li-An Zhou (2009): Microinsurance, Trust and Economic Development: Evidence from a Randomized Natural Field Experiment, PIER Working Paper 09-034, Philadelphia: Penn Institute for Economic Research.

Cameron, Colin A. and Pravin K. Trivedi (2009): *Microeconometrics Using Stata*, First Edition, College Station: Stata Press.

Capellari, Lorenzo and Stephen P. Jenkins (2003): Multivariate Probit Regression Using Simulated Maximum Likelihood, *The Stata Journal*, 3 (3), pp. 278-294.

Cawley, John and Tomas Phillipson (1999): An Empirical Examination of Information Barriers to Trade in Insurance, *American Economic Review*, 89 (4), pp. 827-846.

Chankova, Slavea, Sara Sulzbach and Francois Diop (2008): Impact of Mutual Health Organizations: Evidence from West Africa, *Health Policy and Planning*, 23 (4), pp. 264-276.

Chiappori, Pierre-André (2000): Econometric Models of Insurance Under Asymmetric Information, In *Handbook of Insurance*, edited by G. Dionne. Boston, Dordrecht, London: Kluwer Academic Publishers.

Churchill, Craig (ed.) (2006): *Protecting the Poor. A Micro Insurance Compendium*, Geneva: International Labour Organization (ILO).

Cohen, Monique and Jennefer Sebstad (2003): Financial Education for the Poor, Microfinance Opportunities, Working Paper No. 1.

Cohen, Monique, Michael McCord and Jennefer Sebstad (2005): Reducing Vulnerability: Demand for and Supply of Micro Insurance in East Africa, *Journal of International Development*, 17 (3), pp. 319-325.

Cole, Shawn, Xavier Giné, Jeremy Tobacman, Petia Topalova, Robert M. Townsend and James Vickery (2009): Barriers to Household Risk Management: Evidence from India, Havard Business School Finance Working Paper 09/116, Boston: Harvard Business School.

Coulombe, Harold (2008): Ghana Census - Based Poverty Map: District & Sub-District Level Results, In: *The Economy of Ghana*, edited by E. Aryeetey and R. Kanbur, Accra: Woeli Publishing Services.

Datta, Dipankar (2004): Microcredit in Rural Bangladesh. Is it Reaching the Poorest?, *Journal of Microfinance*, 6 (1), pp. 55-81.

Deaton, Angus (1989): Saving in Developing Countries: Theory and Review, Paper read at World Bank Annual Conference on Development Economics 1989.

Deaton, Angus (1992): Household Saving in LDCs: Credit Markets, Insurance and Welfare, *Scandinavian Journal of Economics*, 94 (2), pp. 253-273.

Dercon, Stefan (2002): Income Risk, Coping Strategies, and Safety Nets, *World Bank Research Observer*, 17 (2), pp. 141-166.

Dercon, Stefan (2004): Risk, Insurance, and Poverty: A Review, In: Stefan Dercon, ed., *Insurance Against Poverty*, Oxford: Oxford University Press.

Dionne, Georges, Neil Doherty, and Nathalie Fombaron (2000): Adverse Selection in Insurance Markets, In: *Handbook of Insurance*, edited by G. Dionne. Boston, Dordrecht, London: Kluwer Academic Publishers.

Dohmen, Thomas J., Armin Falk, David Huffman, Juergen Schupp, Uwe Sunde, and Gert Wagner (2006): Individual Risk Attitudes: New Evidence from a Large, Representative, Experimentally-Validated Survey, CEPR Discussion Paper 5517. London: Centre for Economic Policy Research.

Dror, D.M., R. Radermacher and R. Koren (2007): Willingness to Pay for Health Insurance Among Rural and Poor Persons: Field Evidence from Seven Micro Health Insurance Units in India, *Health Policy*, Vol. 82, No. 1.

Enarsson, Sven and Kjell Wirén (2006): ALMAO and YASIRU Sri Lanka, CGAP Working Group on Microinsurance – Good and Bad Practices – Case Study No 21.

Eswaran, Mukesh and Ashok Kotwal (1989): Credit as Insurance in Agrarian Economies, *Journal of Development Economics*, 31 (1), pp. 37-53.

Fafchamps, Marcel, Christopher Udry and Katherine Czukas (1998): Drought and Saving in West Africa: Are Livestock a Buffer Stock?, *Journal of Development Economics*, 55, pp. 273-305.

Fafchamps, Marcel and Susan Lund (2003): Risk-Sharing Networks in Rural Philippines, *Journal of Development Economics*, 71 (2), pp. 261-287.

Fafchamps, Marcel and F. Gubert (2007): Contingent Loan Repayment in the Philippines, *Economic Development and Cultural Change*, 55 (4), pp. 633-667.

Fafchamps, Marcel and Bart Minten (2007): Public Service Provision, User Fees and Political Turmoil, *Journal of African Economies*, 16 (3), pp. 485-518.

Fischer, Stanley (1973): A Life Cycle Model of Life Insurance Purchases, *International Economic Review*, Vol. 14, No. 1, pp. 132-152.

Friedman, Milton (1957): *A Theory of the Consumption Function*, Princeton: Princeton University Press.

Gant, Richard, Dulan de Silva and Steve Durrant (2004): *Developing Microfinance in the North and East of Sri Lanka*, GTZ/SIDA, Colombo.

Giles, John and Kyeongwan Yoo (2007): Precautionary Behaviour, Migrant Networks, and Household Consumption Decisions: An Empirical Analysis Using Household Panel Data from Rural China, *The Review of Economics and Statistics*, 89 (3), pp. 534-551.

Giné, Xavier, Robert M. Townsend und James Vickery (2008): Patterns of Rainfall Insurance Participation in Rural India, *The World Bank Economic Review*, 22 (3), pp. 539-566.

Giné, Xavier and Dean Yang (2009): Insurance, Credit and Technology Adoption: Field Experimental Evidence from Malawi, *Journal of Development Economics*, 89 (1), pp. 1-11.

Greene, William H. (2003): *Economic Analysis*, Third edition, Upper Saddle River: Prentice Hall.

Gollier, Christian (2003): To Insure or Not to Insure? An Insurance Puzzle, *The Geneva Papers on Risk and Insurance Theory*, 28 (1), pp. 5-24.

GTZ (2009): Microfinance Industry Report Sri Lanka 2009, Produced by GTZ ProMiS in collaboration with The Banking With The Poor Network, Gesellschaft für technische Zusammenarbeit (GTZ): Eschborn.

Guiso, Luigi, Paola Sapienza and Luigi Zingales (2008): Trusting the Stock Market, *Journal of Finance*, 63 (6), pp. 2557-2600.

Gupta, K. L. (1970): Personal Saving in Developing Nations: Further Evidence, *Economic Record*, 46 (2), pp. 243-249.

Gurgand, P., G. Pederson and J. Yaron (1994): Outreach and Sustainability of Six Rural Finance Institutions in Sub-Saharan Africa, Discussion Paper No. 248, Washington DC: World Bank.

Haiss, Peter and Kjell Sümegi (2006): The Relationship of Insurance and Economic Growth – A Theoretical and Empirical Analysis, Paper for Presentation at the 2006 EcoMod Conference, Hongkong, June 28-30, 2006.

Hakansson, Nils H. (1969): Optimal Investment and Consumption Strategies Under Risk, and Uncertain Lifetime and Insurance, *International Economic Review*, 10, pp. 443-466.

Hamid, Syed Abdul, Jennifer Roberts and Paul Mosley (2010): Can Micro Health Insurance Reduce Poverty? Evidence from Bangladesh, Sheffield Economic Research Paper Series, No. 2010001, Sheffield: University of Sheffield.

Handa, Sudhanshu (2002): Raising Primary School Enrolment in Developing Countries, The Relative Importance of Demand and Supply, *Journal of Development Economics*, 69 (1), pp. 103-128.

Heckman, James (1990): Varieties of Selection Bias, *American Economic Review*, Vol. 80, pp. 313-318.

Holzmann, R. and S. Joergensen (2000): Social Risk Management: A New Conceptual Framework for Social Protection, and Beyond, Social Protection Discussion Paper No. 0006, World Bank: Washington DC.

Hong, Harrison, Stanley Kubik and Jeremy Stein (2004): Social Interaction and Stock Market Participation, *Journal of Finance*, 59 (1), pp. 137-163.

Hoogeveen, Johannes (2003): Evidence on Informal Insurance in Rural Zimbabwe, *Journal of African Economies*, 11 (2), pp. 249-278.

Hulme, David and Paul Mosley (1997): Finance for the Poor of the Poorest? Financial Innovations, Poverty and Vulnerability, In: Geoffrey Wood and Iffath Sharif (eds.): *Who Needs Credit? Poverty and Finance in Bangladesh*, Dhaka: University Press, pp. 96-129.

Hurd, Michael D. (1987): Savings of the Elderly and Desired Bequests, *American Economic Review*, 77, pp. 298-312.

Hurd, Michael D. (1994): Measuring the Bequest Motive: The Effect on Children on Saving by the Elderly in the United States, In: Toshiaki Tachibanaki (eds.): *Savings and Bequests*, Michigan: The University of Michigan Press, pp. 111-136.

IMF (2006): Ghana, Poverty Reduction Strategy Paper, IMF Country Report 06/225, Washington DC: International Monetary Fund.

Inkmann, Joachim, Paula Lopes and Alexander Michaelides (2009): How Deep is the Annuity Market Participation Puzzle?, In: Central Bank of Cyprus Working Paper, No. 2009-5, 2009.

Inkmann, Joachim and Alexander Michaelides (2010): Can the Life Insurance Market Provide Evidence for a Bequest Motive?, Working Paper, Central Bank of Cyprus, London School of Economics, 2010.

Ito, Seiro and Hisaki Kono (2010): Why is the Take-Up of Microinsurance so Low? Evidence from a Health Insurance Scheme in India, *The Developing Economies*, 48 (1), pp. 74-101.

Jabbar, M.A., S.K. Ehui and R. von Kaufmann (2002): Supply and Demand for Livestock Credit in Sub-Saharan Africa: Lessons for Designing New Credit Schemes, *World Development*, 30(6), pp. 1029-1042.

Jones, Andrew (2007): *Applied Econometrics for Health Economists: A Practical Guide*, Second Edition, Oxford: Radcliffe Publishing Ltd.

Jütting, Johannes (2003): Do Community-Based Health Insurance Schemes Improve Poor People's Access to Health Care? Evidence From Rural Senegal, *World Development*, 32 (2), pp. 273-288.

Karlan, Dean and Jonathan Morduch (2009): Access to Finance, In: Dani Rodrik and Mark Rosenzweig, eds., *Handbook of Development Economics*, Amsterdam: Elvesier.

Kazianga, Harounan and Christopher Udry (2006): Consumption Smoothing? Livestock, Insurance and Drought in Rural Burkina Faso, *Journal of Development Economics*, 79 (3), pp. 413-446.

Kelley, Allen C., and Jeffrey G. Williamson (1968): Household Saving Behaviour in the Developing Economies: The Indonesian Case, *Economic Development and Cultural Change*, 16 (3), pp. 385-403.

Kempson, Elaine (2009): Framework for the Development of Financial Literacy Baseline Surveys: A First International Comparative Analysis, OECD Working Papers on Finance, Insurance, and Private Pensions, No. 1, OECD Publishing.

Khandker, Shahidur R. (1998): *Fighting Poverty with Microcredit: Experience in Bangladesh*, New York: Oxford University Press for the World Bank.

Kiiza, Barnabas and Glenn Pederson (2002): Household Financial Savings Mobilization: Empirical Evidence from Uganda, *Journal of African Economies*, 10 (4), pp. 390-409.

Kimuyu, Peter Kiko (1999): Rotating Saving and Credit Associations in Rural East Africa, *World Development*, 27 (7), pp. 1299-1308.

Kis-Katos, Krisztina (2007): The Work-Schooling Trade-Off of Indian Children, mimeo.

Kochar, Anjini (1997): An Empirical Investigation of Rationing Constraints in Rural Credit Markets in India, *Journal of Development Economics*, 53 (2), pp. 339-371.

Kurosaki, Takashi and Marcel Fafchamps (2002): Insurance Market Efficiency and Crop Choices in Pakistan, *Journal of Development Economics*, 67 (3), pp. 419-453.

Lafourcade, Anne-Lucie, Jennifer Isern, Patricia Mwangi, and Matthew Brown (2005): Overview of the Outreach and Financial Performance of Microfinance Institutions in Africa, Microfinance Information eXchange (MIX).

Lavy, Victor, John Strauss, Duncan Thomas, and Philippe de Vreyer (1996): Quality of Health Care, Survival and Health Outcomes in Ghana, *Journal of Health Economics*, 15 (3), pp. 333-357.

Lee, Jeong-Joon, and Yasuyuki Sawada (2007): The Degree of Precautionary Saving: A Reexamination, *Economics Letters*, 96 (2), pp. 196-201.

Lee, Jeong-Joon, and Yasuyuki Sawada (2010): Precautionary Saving under Liquidity Constraints: Evidence from Rural Pakistan, *Journal of Development Economics*, 91 (1), pp. 77-86.

Lewis, Frank (1989): Dependents and the Demand for Life Insurance, *American Economic Review*, 79, pp. 452-466.

Lim, Youngjae and Robert M. Townsend (1998): General Equilibrium Models of Financial Systems: Theory and Measurement in Village Economies, *Review of Economic Dynamics*, 1 (1): pp. 59-118.

Loewe, Markus et al. (2001): Improving the Social Protection of the Urban Poor and Near-Poor in Jordan, Reports and Working Paper 12, Bonn: Deutsches Institut für Entwicklungspolitik.

Matul, Michal (2009): Financial Behaviours and Vulnerability to Poverty in Low-Income Households in Transition Context, Microinsurance Innovation Facility, Geneva: ILO.

Matul, Michal, Michael J. McCord, Caroline Phily, and Job Harms (2010): The Landscape of Microinsurance in Africa, Microinsurance Paper 4, Geneva: International Labour Organization.

McCord, Michael J. (2001): Health Care Microinsurance – Case Studies from Uganda, Tanzania, India and Cambodia, *Small Enterprise Development*, 12 (1), pp. 25-38.

McCord, Michael J., Gaby Ramm and Elizabeth McGuinness (2006): Microinsurance. Demand and Market Prospects, Study Commissioned by Allianz, GTZ, United Nations Development Programme (UNDP).

Morduch, Jonathan (1994): Poverty and Vulnerability, *American Economic Review* (AEA Papers and Proceedings), 84 (May), pp. 221-225.

Morduch, Jonathan (1995): Income Smoothing and Consumption Smoothing, *Journal of Economic Perspectives*, 9 (3), pp. 103-114.

Morduch, Jonathan (1999): Between the State and the Market: Can Informal Insurance Patch the Safety Net?, *World Bank Research Observer*, 14 (2), pp. 187-207.

Morduch, Jonathan (2006): Micro-Insurance: The Next Revolution?, In: Ahijit Banerjee, Roland Benabou and Dilip Mookherjee, eds., *Understanding Poverty*, New York: Oxford University Press.

Muradoglu, Gulnur and Fatma Taskin (1996): Differences in Household Savings Behaviour: Evidence from Industrial and Developing Countries, *The Developing Economies*, 34 (2), pp. 138-153.

Navajas, Sergio, M Schreiner, R. L. Meyer, C. Gonzalez-Vega and J. Rodriguez-Meza (2000) : Microcredit and the Poorest of the Poor. Theory and Evidence from Bolivia, *World Development*, 28 (2), pp. 333-346.

Nguyen, Geneviève, Betty Wampfler, Michel Benoit-Cattin and Kimseyinga Savadogo (2002): Characteristics of Household Demand for Financial Services in Highly Uncertain Economies: A Review of Evidence from Burkina Faso, In: Manfred Zeller and Richard L. Meyer (eds.): *The Triangle of Microfinance: Financial Sustainability, Outreach, and Impact*, Washington DC: Johns Hopkins University Press, pp. 46-68.

Outreville, Francois J. (1996): Life Insurance Markets in Developing Countries, *Journal of Risk and Insurance*, 63, pp. 263-278.

Pal, Sarmistha (2002): Household Sectoral Choice and Effective Demand for Rural Credit in India, *Applied Economics*, 14, pp. 1743-1755.

Pauly, M.V. (2004): The Demand for Health Insurance: Insights from Theory and Voluntary Markets in Less-Developed Countries, Background paper presented at Wharton Impact Conference on Voluntary Health Insurance in Developing Countries, March 15-16, University of Pennsylvania, http://hc.wharton.upenn.edu/impactconference/index.html (accessed on 07.11.2008).

Pissarides, C.A. (1980): The Wealth - Age Relation with Life Insurance, *Economica*, 47, pp. 451-457.

Pitt, Mark M. and Shahidur R. Khandker (2002): Credit Programmes for the Poor and Seasonality in Rural Bangladesh, *Journal of Development Studies*, 39 (2), pp. 1-24.

Platteau, Jean-Philippe (1997): Mutual Insurance as an Elusive Concept in Traditional Rural Communities, *Journal of Development Studies*, 33 (6), pp. 764-796.

Pratt, J. (1964): Risk Aversion in the Small and in the Large, *Econometrica*, 32, pp. 122-136.

Private Finance Research Centre (PFRC) (2005): Measuring Financial Capability: An Explanatory Study, Prepared for Financial Services Authority by Personal Finance Research Centre, University of Bristol.

Radermacher, Ralf, Iddo Dror and Gerry Noble (2006): Challenges and Strategies to Extend Health Insurance to the Poor, In: Churchill, C. (ed.), *Protecting the Poor, A Microinsurance compendium*, International Labor Organisation, Geneva.

Rajivan, Anuradha (2007): Proceedings of the Regional Workshop on Microinsurance Sector Development, June 2007: Building Security for the Poor – Potential and Prospects for Microinsurance in India, Colombo.

Ray, Debraj (1999): *Development Economics*, Princeton: University Press.

Republic of Ghana (2007): Patterns and Trends of Poverty in Ghana 1991 – 2006, Accra: Ghana Statistical Service.

Roth, Jim, Michael McCord and Dominic Liber (2007): The Landscape of Microinsurance in the World's 100 Poorest Countrie, The Microinsurance Centre: LLC.

Rothschild, Michael and Joseph E. Stiglitz (1976): Equilibrium in Competitive Insurance Markets: An Essay on the Economics of Imperfect Information, *Quarterly Journal of Economics*, 90, pp. 630-49.

Rutherford, Stuart (1999): *The Poor and Their Money*, Institute for Development Policy and Management, University of Manchester.

Schindler, K. (2010): Credit for What? Informal Credit as a Coping Strategy of Market Women in Northern Ghana, *Journal of Development Studies*, 46 (2), pp. 234-253.

Schneider, Pia (2005): Trust in Micro-Health Insurance: an Exploratory Study in Rwanda, *Social Science and Medicine*, Vol. 61, pp. 1430-38.

Siegel, Paul B., Jeffrey Alwang and Sudharshan Canagarajah (2001): Viewing Microinsurance as a Social Risk Management Instrument, Social Protection Discussion Paper No. 0116, World Bank: Washington DC.

Skinner, Jonathan (1988): Risky Income, Life Cycle Consumption, and Precautionary Saving, *Journal of Monetary Economics*, 22 (2), pp. 237-255.

Spio, K. and J.A. Groenewald (1996): Rural Household Savings and the Life Cycle Hypotheses: The Case of South Africa, *The South African Journal of Economics*, 64, pp. 294-304.

Steel, William, and David Andah (2008): Rural and Microfinance Regulation in Ghana: Implications for Development of the Industry, In: *The Economy of Ghana*, edited by E. Aryeetey and R. Kanbur, Accra: Woeli Publishing Services.

Swain, Ranjula Bali (2002): Credit Rationing in Rural India, *Journal of Economic Development*, 27(2), pp. 1-20.

The Department of Census & Statistics (2008): Sri Lanka Demographic and Health Survey 2006/7, Preliminary Report, The Department of Census & Statistics: Colombo.

Thornton, Rebecca, Erica Field, Laurel Hyatt, Mursaleena Islam, and Freddy Solis (2009): Social Security Health Insurance for the Informal Sector in Nicaragua: A Randomized Evaluation, Mimeo.

Tilakaratna, G. (2005): Impact of Micro-Credit on Selected Household Welfare Attributes: Evidence from Sri Lanka, Microfinance Gateway, CGAP/ World Bank, Washington D.C.

Tomes, Nigel (1982): The Family, Inheritance, and the Intergenerational Transmission of Inequality, *Journal of Political Economy*, 89, pp. 928-958.

Townsend, Robert (1995): Consumption Insurance: An Evaluation of Risk-Bearing Systems in Low-Income Economies, *Journal of Economic Perspectives*, 9 (3), pp. 83-102.

Truett, Dale B. and Lila J. Truett (1990): The Demand for Life Insurance in Mexico and the United States: A Comparative Study, *Journal of Risk and Insurance*, 57, pp. 321-328.

Vanderpuye-Orgle, J. and C. B. Barrett (2009): Risk Management and Social Visibility in Ghana, *African Development Review*, 21 (1), pp. 5-35.

Vidal-Meliá, Carlos and Ana Lejárraga-Garcia (2005): The Bequest Motive and Single People's Demand for Life Annuities, *The Belgian Actuarial Bulletin*, Vol. 4, pp. 4-15.

Walliser, Jan and Joachim K. Winter (1998): Tax Incentives, Bequest Motives and the Demand for Life Insurance: Evidence from Germany, Working Paper No. 99-28, University of Mannheim, 1998.

Wang, Holly H. and Robert Rosenman (2007): Preceived Need and Actual Demand for Health Insurance Among Rural Chinese Residents, *China Economic Review*, 18 (4), pp. 373-388.

Waters, H. (1999): Measuring the Impact of Health Insurance with a Correction for Selection Bias a Case Study of Ecuador, *Health Economics and Econometrics*, 8, pp. 473-483.

Winter, Ralph (2000): Optimal Insurance Under Moral Hazard, In: *Handbook of Insurance*, edited by G. Dionne. Boston, Dordrecht, London: Kluwer Academic Publishers.

Witter, Sophie and Bertha Garshong (2009): Something Old or Something New? Social Health Insurance in Ghana, *BMC International Health and Human Rights*, 9: 1-10.

World Bank (2008): *Finance for All? Policies and Pitfalls in Expanding Access*, World Bank Policy Research Report, Washington DC: World Bank.

Yaari, Menahem E. (1965): Uncertain Lifetime, Life Insurance, and the Theory of the Consumer, *Review of Economic Studies*, 32, pp. 137-150.

Yunus, Muhammad (2003): *Banker to the Poor: Micro-Lending and the Battle Against World Poverty*, Public Affairs: New York.

Zeldes, Stephen (1989): Consumption and Liquidity Constraints, An Empirical Investigation, *Journal of Political Economy*, 97 (2), pp. 305-346.

Zelizer, Viviana A. Rotman (1979): *Morals and Markets: The Development of Life Insurance in the United States*, New York, NY: Columbia University Press.

Zeller, Manfred (2001): The Safety Net Role of Microfinance for Income and Consumption Smoothing, In: Nora Lustig (ed.): *Shielding the Poor. Social Protection in the Developing World*, Washington DC: Brookings Institution and Inter-American Development Bank, pp. 217-238.

Zeller, Manfred and Manohar Sharma (2002): Access to and Demand for Financial Services by the Rural Poor: A Multicountry Synthesis, In: Manfred Zeller and Richard L. Meyer (eds.): *The Triangle of Microfinance: Financial Sustainability, Outreach, and Impact*, Baltimore and London: Johns Hopkins University Press, pp. 19-45.

Göttinger Studien zur Entwicklungsökonomik
Göttingen Studies in Development Economics

Herausgegeben von / Edited by Hermann Sautter
und / and Stephan Klasen

Die Bände 1-8 sind über die Vervuert Verlagsgesellschaft (Frankfurt/M.) zu beziehen.

Bd. / Vol. 9 Hermann Sautter / Rolf Schinke (eds.): Social Justice in a Market Economy. 2001.

Bd. / Vol. 10 Philipp Albert Theodor Kircher: Poverty Reduction Strategies. A comparative study applied to empirical research. 2002.

Bd. / Vol. 11 Matthias Blum: Weltmarktintegration, Wachstum und Innovationsverhalten in Schwellenländern. Eine theoretische Diskussion mit einer Fallstudie über „Argentinien 1990-1999". 2003.

Bd. / Vol. 12 Jan Müller-Scheeßel: Die Privatisierung und Regulierung des Wassersektors. Das Beispiel Buenos Aires / Argentinien. 2003.

Bd. / Vol. 13 Ludger J. Löning: Economic Growth, Biodiversity Conservation, and the Formation of Human Capital in a Developing Country. 2004.

Bd. / Vol. 14 Silke Woltermann: Transitions in Segmented Labor Markets. The Case of Brazil. 2004.

Bd. / Vol. 15 Jörg Stosberg: Political Risk and the Institutional Environment for Foreign Direct Investment in Latin America. An Empirical Analysis with a Case Study on Mexico. 2005.

Bd. / Vol. 16 Derk Bienen: Die politische Ökonomie von Arbeitsmarktreformen in Argentinien. 2005.

Bd. / Vol. 17 Dierk Herzer: Exportdiversifizierung und Wirtschaftswachstum. Das Fallbeispiel Chile. 2006.

Bd. / Vol. 18 Jann Lay: Poverty and Distributional Impact of Economic Policies and External Shocks. Three Case Studies from Latin America Combining Macro and Micro Approaches. 2007.

Bd. / Vol. 19 Kenneth Harttgen: Empirical Analysis of Determinants, Distribution and Dynamics of Poverty. 2007.

Bd. / Vol. 20 Stephan Klasen / Felicitas Nowak-Lehmann: Poverty, Inequality and Migration in Latin America. 2008.

Bd. / Vol. 21 Isabel Günther: Empirical Analysis of Poverty Dynamics. With Case Studies from Sub-Saharan Africa. 2007.

Bd. / Vol. 22 Peter Dung: Malaysia und Indonesien: Wirtschaftliche Entwicklungsstrategien in zwei Vielvölkerstaaten. 2008.

Bd. / Vol. 23 Thomas Otter: Poverty, Income Growth and Inequality in Paraguay During the 1990s. Spatial Aspects, Growth Determinants and Inequality Decomposition. 2008.

Bd. / Vol. 24 Mark Misselhorn: Measurement of Poverty, Undernutrition and Child Mortality. 2008.

Bd. / Vol. 25 Julian Weisbrod: Growth, Poverty and Inequality Dynamics. Four Empirical Essays at the Macro and Micro Level. 2008.

Bd. / Vol. 26 Johannes Gräb: Econometric Analysis in Poverty Research. With Case Studies from Developing Countries. 2009.

Bd. / Vol. 27 Sebastian Vollmer: A Contribution to the Empirics of Economic and Human Development. 2009.

Bd. / Vol. 28 Wokia-azi Ndangle Kumase: Aspects of Poverty and Inequality in Cameroon. 2010.

Bd. / Vol. 29 Adriana Rocío Cardozo Silva: Economic Growth and Poverty Reduction in Colombia. 2010.

Bd. / Vol. 30 Ronald Kröker: Ansätze zur Implementierung von RSE (CSR) in einem lateinamerikanischen Entwicklungsland. Das Beispiel Paraguay – Eine wirtschafts- und unternehmensethische Untersuchung. 2010.

Bd. / Vol. 31 Maria Ziegler: Institutions, Inequality and Development. 2011.

Bd. / Vol. 32 Melanie Grosse: Measurement of Trends in Wellbeing, Poverty, and Inequality with Case Studies from Bolivia and Colombia. 2011.

Bd. / Vol. 33 Boris Branisa Caballero: Social Institutions, Gender Inequality, and Regional Convergence in Developing Countries. 2012.

Bd. / Vol. 34 Mirko Bendig: Empirical Analysis of Participation Patterns in Microfinancial Markets. The Cases of Ghana and Sri Lanka. 2012.

www.peterlang.de